WHO RAISED HIM

WHO RAISED HIM

Larry Luv

Who Raised Him

Copyright © 2022 by Larry Luv. All rights reserved.

No part of this publication may be reproduced, stored in a retrieval system or transmitted in any way by any means, electronic, mechanical, photocopy, recording or otherwise without the prior permission of the author except as provided by USA copyright law.

This is a Biography, and all the discretions, entities, and incidents in the story are true.

The opinions expressed by the author are not necessarily those of URLink Print and Media.

1603 Capitol Ave., Suite 310 Cheyenne, Wyoming USA 82001
1-888-980-6523 | admin@urlinkpublishing.com

URLink Print and Media is committed to excellence in the publishing industry.

Book design copyright © 2022 by URLink Print and Media. All rights reserved.

Published in the United States of America

Library of Congress Control Number: 2022902796
ISBN 978-1-68486-096-8 (Paperback)
ISBN 978-1-68486-096-8 (Digital)

13.04.21

INTRODUCTION

I write this book on behalf of my mother, Mrs. Ethel Mae Coldwell, and my brothers, Johnny Kaye and Gregory Coldwell, as well as my childhood friends like Douglas Mabry and many others who died living life in Harlem during the 1960s-1987, when we were in a drug war and did not have any idea that we were at war with nothing to fight with.

My name Larry was given to me by a white nurse in Sumter, South Carolina in 1952, when my mother who could not read was given a bottle of poison to take by the doctor while in labor, with the instructions *"when you start having labor pains take this medicine."* When my mother began feeling the labor pains from me, she called the nurse and asked her to give her the medicine in that bottle and the nurse said, "This is poison and you can't take it, honey." On the bottle was a skeleton head with arms crossed which the nurse pointed out to my mother, and she learned from that experience how to recognize a bottle of poison. My mother gave her the right to name me as her appreciation for saving both our lives. The nurse named me Larry which means loyalty.

Larry Love God was known as a crazy Mother Hubbard from 122nd Street, and he spent most of his life in and out of institutions and jails to prison. Most of his life was lived climbing the rough side of life's mountains as he lived in a very unfair social system.

Larry Love God was born to die, like every living things are born to die, and continues to live in the middle of that life and shadowing death journey as he now posed the question to all of us: Who raised Larry, Loves God?

LARRY'S STORY: WHO RAISED HIM

I now look back on my walk through this life journey and so many of my sisters, brothers and childhood friends tour of this life. I now ask the question "what is it all about, and what is its purpose for me and humanity to travel such and up and down life journey".

By
Larry Moses Coldwell

CHAPTER 1

I recall saying to my mother, Ma please don't let them take me away. I was crying my eyes out at 8 years old while sitting on the Bellevue hospital bus at 24th Street and first avenue on the East side of downtown Manhattan heading to Rockland State mental health facility for children.

I did not understand what had happen to me. As I looked out of the bus window there was my mother crying her eyes out as well. I did not want to put this story in my book because it is a situation that I have been ashamed of since the day it happened in 1960.

What lead to me being in Bellevue was on one school day in the second grade at PS 81 on 119 Street between St. Nicolas and 7th avenue, I went into class and attempted to sit in my assigned seat when someone eased the chair from under me causing me to fall flat on my butt. Everyone in the class room seemed to have gotten a good laugh out of me falling on my butt; hell, I even laughed myself. So here comes one of my female classmates entering the class room preparing to sit down and I eased the chair from under her just like it was done to me and she fell down on her butt, and I don't recall anyone laughing at her like they laughed at me. Needles to say, she broke her arm and the next thing I know, I was in the crazy house in Bellevue Hospital at 8 years old.

I recall seeing a therapist in Bellevue; it seemed like every week and he would ask me "do you hear voices or see images of things" and I would say no because I never heard any voices and the only images I ever saw was when I was home sleeping in the middle of the bed with my younger brothers Kaye, Greg and Pee Nut. I slept in the middle because I was scared of this image I often saw at night when my mother put us to bed and the lights were out. It was actually my mother's winter coat hanging on the back of our bedroom door that lead to the kitchen. The door was close at knight to keep the rats in the kitchen, and out of our bedroom. Our room was adjacent to the kitchen and those rats were some bad mothers. So the coat hanging there at night would scare the hell out of me whenever I awake at night. That's the only image I had ever seen at 8 years old and the only voice I had ever heard was when my mother would tell me she was going to beat my butt with that ironing cord for misbehaving.

So, here I am in Bellevue hospital mental health ward for what I never could understand and this white man would keep asking me if I hear voices or see images every time I saw him. He also had me play with some cards with dark images on them and he would ask me "what does it look like to you". There were lots of kids there in my age group and most of them seem to be a lot like me, so we would play and run around the nut house every day. I often would sit and look out the window hoping to see my mother and hoping she would take me back home. She came to visit me but not to take me home. I would cry and plead with her to take me home and she would cry her eyes out and say "I can't son." One day I went to see the therapist and he asked me the same dam questions about voices and images and I was mad about something so this time I said to him "yes, I hear voices and see images." And the next thing I know I was boarding this bus heading to some place called Rockland State in 1960. Rockland State was known as the crazy house in Harlem and I could not understand why I was being sent there. I recall being put in a big room with about 20 or more kids my age there at Rockland State, and someone told me they have skunks around outside. I was scared as hell because the only Skunk, I ever knew about was Winnie the Pooh. I recall when we would go to the cafeteria to eat and none of us would eat the mashed potatoes because it was nasty. They would force us to eat it, and also when we misbehaved they would strip us butt naked and wrap us up in a white sheet like a mummy and place us in the middle of the bed with large blocks of ice around us. They called it Cold Sheeting. They would make us lie there for hours until the ice melted. Whenever, I was cold sheeted I would lay there and relate to Humphrey Bogart or Edward G. Robinson movies and how they dealt with situations in the movies that was unfair to them. Relating to the movies helped me to deal with the cold sheeting experience. I don't know just how long I was in Rockland State; maybe six months or less before I was sent home.

From that experience my life, began to evolve and take on a mean role. I became a "kick ass nigger" and if anyone got in my way I would fight like a crazy man to scare the hell out of the on lookers to keep them from messing with me. As I look back on that experience today, I wonder was I crazy enough at 8 years old to be sent to the crazy house. My poor mother would visit me during those months and cry her heart out during the visit.

I don't know why or how it happened, but looking back on my life then, my brother Kaye and I took to the streets of New York City as children like a fish in water. I recall when our mother was crying one day when we lived on 60th Street between 10th and 11th avenue in the late 1950s; The white Gangsters would drive speeding through our block shooting at each other just like in the Humphrey Bogart movies. Kaye and I would dive into the basement so that we would not get shot by the white gangsters that were shooting at each other. Well, on this particular day I was about 6 years old and Kaye was 5 years old and our mother was crying her heart out about something and when I asked her why she was crying she said that she did not have rent money to pay the rent. Kaye and I learned how much rent money she needed and the both of us went outside and hustled up the money, by way of begging and stole whatever we could that night from the stores down town. Kaye and I would steal from the stores that had it all, every chance we got. We gave the money to our mother and she no longer had a rent problem. From that day until I was 35 years old, my life was nothing but a street hustle to survive.

CHAPTER 2

In 1958 after living in Hell's Kitchen we moved to Spanish Harlem on 115th Street between 5th and Madison Avenue. Kaye and I stole like hell from the Park Avenue stores. We lived with our mother, 3 sisters and 2 other brothers. My younger brother Pee Nut was the baby and one day our father caught up with us. My mother left him in Brooklyn with his family and moved us to Hell's kitchen to Spanish Harlem. One day, after finding us in Spanish Harlem, my father Moies, tried to take Pee Nut with him by putting him in a shopping bag at about 10 months old. He was coming out of the building with Pee Nut. My sister Doris was walking out of the building with him and when she saw our mother, she called out to her and told her "Ma, he got Pee Nut in the shopping bag." Moies slapped Doris and told her to shut the hell up. My mother questioned Moies and he began to get violent with my mother but the guy who worked in the News stand on the corner of 115 Street and Fifth avenue pulled out a shot gun and made Moies drop the shopping bag with Pee Nut in it. Afterwards we did not see Moies for years. The building we lived in on the corner of 115th Street between 5th and Madison Avenue was connected to the News stand. Our family shared a railroad flat apartment with about five other families and we all shared the one bathroom and kitchen. I remember one of our neighbors in our apartment tried to use our pots and pans and my sisters Doris,

Rosetta and I had jumped him and beat him up for using our pots and pans. Doris is one year older than Rosetta and two years older than me. I believe I was about 8 years old when we jumped that grown man who was a wino. For the most part we got along with the other families that shared the apartment with us and we ended up calling each other cousins. My mother met Boose when we lived in Hell's Kitchen, whose real name was Sylvia Smith. She became our aunt and family supporter along with her 4 children up until her death in 1980.

    My mother struggled to raise her seven children alone in Big New York City, as she was an abused country girl with no academic education, but she had very strong survival skills. I think she developed her skills when she was a little girl and had to sleep in the middle of her mother and her mother's white husband in South Carolina during the 1940s. As a result my mother gave birth to two girls Elisabeth and Carolyn of whom I knew nothing about. The story is told that my father's father took my mother from that abusive situation. My mother told me that my father's father was so mean until he could climb a tree backwards. However, my mother was a survivor and she made sure my six siblings and I had everything we needed. She also gave the same level of care to her new six children making my sisters and brothers 12 children in total with a single parent. In 1960, when I was 8 years old, we moved to 122nd Street; wherein for the first time we had our own apartment since moving to New York City. I remember being on the moving truck and crying because we were leaving 115th Street. I remember when we moved into a building on 122nd Street, building 244 apartment 6 on the third floor and three buildings from 8th avenue on the even number side of the street. It was about our second day living in 122nd street in the afternoon around 5PM in July and my mother sent Doris, Rosetta, Kaye and I to the laundry on 123rd St. and 8th avenue. We had just moved into the block and had about 9 pillow cases of laundry. We took the first load down stairs and set it on the stoop to go back upstairs to get the rest of the laundry, and when we came back down stairs our laundry was thrown into the basement. There were about 5 kids from the block standing on the side laughing at us. Doris called up to the window to my mother and when she came to the window, Doris said "Ma, look what they did", and my mother said " get them", Doris, Rosetta, Kaye and I went at them like a bunch of wild bears. From that day on everyone in 122nd Street knew that if you messed with the Coldwell's they will fight you back. I don't recall fighting in Hell's Kitchen and only that one fight over our pots in Spanish Harlem; however, from that day on I would fight like a crazy mother to send the message to everyone that if you mess with me I am going to fight like hell with you. It was at that point that I began to hate my father Moies for not being in our lives to protect us and leaving me there to be the one who had to fight like a crazy man to protect my sisters and brothers. I hated fighting because I was more attracted to the girls at an early age and I liked playing with them, not fighting with guys.

There was an A&P Super market between 123rd and 124th Street and 8th avenue on the uptown side of the street; Kaye and I would go there to steal pints of ice cream to eat. We would sit on the stoop eating it causing all the kids to come look at us eating it. They wanted some of the ice cream so badly. We began to meet our peers in 122nd Street. Ronald and Douglas who were brothers living in building 260 next to my building and Robert, Donna and Tony were from building 230 in the block heading towards 7th avenue. We would run together just like the Little Rascals and steal everything we got our hands on. We never stole from our block and community. We would go to Macys, Saks, Gambles and Chains downtown on 34th Street and 14th Street and steal, like hell. Our poor mothers would have to come get us from the precinct when we got caught in places like Staten Island, Long Island, Queens, the Bronx and Brooklyn at nine years old. I believe

I started going to the Youth House facility for troubled youth in the Bronx at the age of ten years old always for stealing from stores. One thing I learned in the Youth House is they would assign 3 of the youth as counselors; there was counselor 1, counselor 2, and counselor number 3. They would tell the rest of us when to line up and when to go into our one person room or whatever the house man wanted to relay to us troubled youth. I would pick a fight with counselor number three, beat him up and take his position as a counselor and from there I would work my way to become counselor number 1.

The Youth House was for mischievous male and female youth. My brother Kaye, Robert, Tony, Doug and I, spent lots of months in there as youth.

CHAPTER 3

At about 12 years old I got tired of my mother having to pick Kaye and I up from the Precinct at the same time so I stopped hanging with him. Kaye was in Children Village at 12 years old and my mother and I would go visit him; the next thing I knew my mother talked me into agreeing to be enlisted there also. I was there for about 6 months or less and learned how to tie a shirt tie. I also remember running away from Children Village in Dobbs Ferry Yonkers, New York about every other week. I don't remember the name of the cottage I was housed in, but I knew it faced the woods and I would sneak out of the cottage back door and go into the woods. After about 20 minutes in the woods and down a big hill I would walk the highway then onto the train tracks heading south towards Manhattan. One day when I ran away and walked through the woods I ran into a bus stop and hustled up bus fare to ride the bus straight to Manhattan. Once I got to Manhattan I was safe and knew how to make it to Harlem. All the times I ran away from Children Village I would go to Kaye's cottage and ask him if he wanted to run away with me and he would say no. I would run by myself every now and then a few guys would go with me but most of the times I would run away by myself and every time I made it home my mother would call Children Village to come take me back; I was never caught running away from Children Village. The last time I ran away and was sent back to Children Village and when I looked up, I was once again in Bellevue Hospital with some white man asking me do I hear voices or see visions. I was about 13 years old in Bellevue Hospital again; because I kept running away from Children Village. I sucked my thumb all my life and nothing my mother or anyone could do to get me to stop sucking my thumb. Well, on my second day in Bellevue for the second time I was sucking my thumb my second morning there and this guy I was talking to said "Larry if they see you sucking your finger they are going to fuck you." I was in a housing area with guys in their late teenage age group. Well that was my last time ever sucking my thumb in my life after my friend told me that. I knew that I was bad and would steal from any white man that had everything I nor anyone in my community had on earth. I know that when I got angry I would go buck wild, but did I really belong in Bellevue again for running away from Children Village, a place that I volunteered to be in. Bellevue cafeteria had some good hamburgers and when my mother came to visit me she would give me money to buy a hamburger. As faith would have it one day I bought a hamburger and sat it down to go to the bathroom and when I came back there was a big bite out of it. This older guy about 16 years old was on the side with his friends chewing my burger and laughing. Well, I went buck wild at him and was fighting him like a mad man and the next thing I knew I was in a straight jacket and back in Rockland State house. They no longer Cold Sheeted, now 5 years later, but when we misbehaved they would give you a shot of Thorazine and that would put you out cold for the rest of the day and I got that shot once. What I could not understand was how is it that I volunteered to go to Children Village and from running away from children village I ended up in Bellevue to Rockland State again. Well, I only stayed in Rockland State for about 90 days and was sent home.

    I was not a thinker as a youth, I was more a re-actionist. No one had ever told me or taught me how to stop and think before I act. So during my youth when a situation happened I would respond to it without taking time to stop and think. I had no known ambitions because in my world there was nothing but Pimps, Number runners, and Drug dealers and the only working men were the few that worked in the Garment district. I recall the Garment district workers would take a lunch bag to work with a bottle of wine in it. When I watched TV, all I saw was white people living a life that no Black people I knew were living in the 50s-60s from sports too movies. I had no idea what I wanted to become during my youth; I could not read and stayed away from games like Monopoly because you had to read the Stay out of Jail cards. Therefore my goal in life was to steal from White folks stores because they had everything I did not have and wanted.

So, here I was home from the nut house. Some of the guys from my block attempted to call me Captain Larry from the Coco House and I cut that short by letting everyone know that I would fight like hell if you called me that name; so they said it behind my back and made damn sure I never got a hint of it being said. It was not that I was so tough that people would avoid fighting with me, it is that they knew that I would fight like hell and I had a good punch. In 1965, I became a Five 5 Per-Centers at the age of 13, which is a lot like Islam. Well after being kicked out of school for not going to school and I started hanging out with the 5 Per-Centers, and the next thing I know is that I had a crew of 5 Per-Centers, and I said to them, guys lets go hit this store on 147 street and Third Avenue in the Bronx, and one of them said Okay Akbar that sounds like a good spot to hit. Third Avenue in the Bronx had lots of stores like downtown Manhattan and 125th street. I was A Poor Righteous Teachers (5 Per-Center) name Akbar in 1966, and the name means (Akbar built the Arch to place upon Righteousness). You had better know your mathematics in the early 1960s. I had a crew of about 5 other Five Per-Centers from the age of 10 years old to 14 years old. I was the leader and the body guard for the group.

One day while stealing from the store in the Bronx the police got onto us and we had to run for it. The police was closing in on the youngest member of our gang and about to catch him until I cut across the police chasing him and drawing the attention to me. Well the police focused his attention on me and I got caught and was sent to the Youth House in 1966. A group of guys and I escaped from the Youth house after being there for about two months. It was about six of us and we had one Counselor watching us along with about 20 other troubled youth. Someone had gotten hold of a wire cutter and while we was working on the window cutting our way out the 20 guys was all around the Counselor making lots of noise to block out what we were doing. About six of us made it out of that window on the first floor and we went on a stealing spree for about five hours. I made it home and once again the police came to my mother's house and I found myself back in the Youth House by way of the police taking me back. From the Youth House I was sent to Warwick State Training School. I remember while in Warwick I did not know how to read and a Spanish friend name Negron and I agreed that he would read my mail for me and in return I would beat up anyone who messed with him. One day after class this Black male teacher at Warwick held me until everyone had left the class room and he said to me "Larry, you don't know how to read do you." That was the first time in my 14 years of life that anyone ever asked me that question. When I was home in 122nd Street and my age group would be playing games like Monopoly or Scrabble and ask me, Larry come play with us, I would respond I don't play those Sissy games. I was often kicked out of school or placed in the back of the class room where the teacher never challenged me to do anything in class but be quiet. One thing I did was also travel to school carrying lots of books presenting the image that I could read them, but I did not know how to read and it seemed like no one cared because no one ever challenged me or asked me if I could read. So here I stood in a class room in Warwick State training school with this Black male teacher challenging me for the first time in my life. I answered his question honestly with a resounding "no, I can't read" and he said to me "Larry, would you like to learn how to read" and I said "yes". He and I agreed on a school schedule that the two of us would be in the class room together as he taught me how to read and within a few months I was reading just as good as everyone else in my age group, and I received a trophy for reading and have been reading every sense. I learned how to tie a tie while in Children village and stopped sucking my thumb in Bellevue for the second time, and how to read in Warwick State training school.

CHAPTER 4

I was kicked out of Warwick State Training School for threatening to beat up my house manager, and I was sent to the Annex State Training School in upstate New York on April 16, 1967. I threaten to beat up the House Manager because he told me he was not going to recommend that I be released when I have my release hearing. My hearing for release was coming up after being there for six months. Well after spending 5 months there and 5 months in the Youth House before I was sent to Warwick and now I am being sent to the Annex State Training School in 1967. They sent me to lock up and from there I was sent to the Annex State Training School where I served 13 months incarcerated for telling the house manager at Warwick that I will beat him up if he does not recommend parole for me.

    I met a brother from Buffalo while in Annex State Training School, and he would say "Hey Larry you up"? "Yes, Sap what's up?" "Nothing man, I just want you to tell me some more about Harlem man". "Okay my man; what time is it Sap?", "about 8pm". I would tell him about my life growing up in Harlem.

    Well, back home about this time I would be out on a Friday night looking for a house party. Most of the times, I rolled by myself because my gang was too young to hang with me that late at night. Anyway I would have received the information on a party earlier in the week. They always passed out index cards with the party information on them. The card would say something like "Martha's house party Friday night at 167 West 114th street and Lenox Avenue from 8pm to 12pm, 25 cents in advance and 35 cents at the door. Hot dogs and soda's for sale. Armed with this information I would get clean, with my tailor made silk pants that I would buy the material from Delancey street and take it to the tailor called Mr. Toni on 125th Street between 7th and Lenox avenue to have my pants tailor made. My shirts was from A.J. Lester store on 125 Street and 8th avenue (up from the Apollo Theater) and a pair of Playboy shoes on my feet, and my pocket full of cash and a couple of $3 bags of reefer. Man, the party did not start until I got there. When I went to a party I would look around at all the girls. Most times it's real hard to see in those party's because the red lights were very dark. Anyway, by the time I saw a girl I like, I would slide over to where the records were and find my main man Smokey Robinson. I got the person spinning the records to play Smokey and then I'd slide up beside my target waiting for Smokey to play. As soon as Smokey started singing "Baby Come Close, Oh Baby, Baby and Quiet Storm" I would reach for the girls hand and say very softly would you like to dance; and she would say yes. Then I'd walk her to the middle of the floor and start slow grinding with her. Yo, Sap, I don't let her head lay on my shoulder because she had that grease in her hair and that stuff would mess up my AJ Lester shirt. So I would grind with my right side of my face to hers as I whisper sweet sounds of Smokey's song in her ear. Before the song was over I would have her name and address and for the rest of the party she would be hanging with me. The two of us would ease outside smoke some joints then go back and party hard.

    I did not like hanging out on my block much back then, but I did have my girl in the block. We called her Pipes because she was a healthy, skinny, and fine red bone. No matter what, Pipes was my girl and she is waiting for me to come home now. "Yo, Sap, I'm going to bed I'll see you tomorrow" Ok Larry, I like to hear about Harlem and one day I am going to tell you about Buffalo.

"Yo, Larry, what's happening." Nothing, Eddie I hear you telling that Buffalo country boy about sweet old Harlem". Man you got me thinking about home. Yo, Larry, when we get out I'm going to take you uptown to 147th street where I live. Yeah, I hear you Eddie but 122nd is the very heart of Harlem and I love that block and everyone that lives on it. I hear you Larry but you have to try uptown, it's where all the tough guys live and we party hard uptown. I tell you what Eddie when we go home I'll hang up your way and then you hang down mine, deal? That's a deal Larry. See you later baby, later man.

Hey what's up Larry? Not much Sap; it was hard for me to sleep last night, you had me thinking about my Pipes all night. I had to jerk off last night so that I could get to sleep.

Damn it's hot in this yard, yes Sap it is. Yo, Larry, you want to play paddle ball? Yeah okay. Damn here come this dumb Brooklyn chump Herm. I did not get along with Herm and every time we met up he wanted to fight me. Yo Larry, why does he always want to fight you? Damn if I know Sap. Yo Manhattan punk what you and this country nigger talking about me for. Look nigger, get your broke Brooklyn dumb ass out of my face. Come on Larry don't fight this fool today. Yeah Larry, go on with your punk ass. Sap move out my way this chump needs his butt kicked.

Hey you two guys stop fighting. I'm not stopping until I kick this Brooklyn nigger's ass back to Brooklyn, let me go get the fuck out of my way. Beat his ass Larry. You Harlem punks can't fight.

I said break it up you two Herm go to your block before I put you in the hole. Mr. Smith he started it. Let me go Mr. Smith; Coldwell you had better calm down before you go to the hole. Fuck the hole I'm going to kill that punk for hitting me in my face. Mr. Smith said boy if you don't calm down I'm going to put you in the hole. Damn once again here I am in this hole. Hell with it, if Jimmy Cagney could handle it I can too. But damn this hole with these four dull walls of gray with this concrete floor and toilet with no seat. I'm glad it's not winter that seat is cold as hell and I'll be glad when 8PM comes, so I can get a piece of mattress and canvas blanket. I wonder if there ever were blankets. "Chow time Coldwell get up and get this food". "What is it? It's bacon, eggs and orange juice; Yo, slide it through. Excuse me but has my counselor been told that I'm here and that I want to see him? Yes your counselor Mr. Shivery knows you're here and he will come see you when he gets a chance. Okay thanks. Say what time do I have to give the mattress and blanket back? At 8am. And what time is it now 6am? "Damn how did I let myself get out of control again", I hope this does not mess my chances up for release next month when I go to the release hearing committee. Okay Coldwell let's get that mattress and blanket out here. Damn now I have to lay on this cold hard floor. I sure hope Mr. Shivery will come early and get me out of this hole. Boy I sure miss 122nd Street. For me there's no place like Harlem especially 122nd Street. I love that block and everyone on it so much. I hope I get a shot to go home at the hearing next month. Now that I'll be 16 years old next month, I'm a man now and when I get out I'm going to make lots of money. Coldwell, Coldwell, yes, Mr. Shivery, I'm right here. Come on out here, didn't I tell you to stay out of trouble? Yes Mr. Shivery, but that chump hit me first. Yes, I learned that but Larry you must learn how to calm down. I know and believe me I try Mr. Shivery. I know you're trying Larry it's just that you are going to have to try harder. Well thank God they just put you in the hole to get you to calm down so this does not go on your record. You know you go to the hearing in May of next month, yes Mr. Shivery. And what I would like to know is, what are my chances of going home? Well you've been here eleven months now and we really have not had any real problems with you wanting to beat up any of our staff like at Warwick State Training School; so it looks good for you if you don't mess it up between now and then. So go on up to your unit and stay out of trouble. By the way Larry what unit are you in? I'm in wing five.

Larry, I'm glad you're out of the hole man. Thanks Sap. Yo Larry you're out of the hole; yeah, Eddie they only had me in there to calm me down. Did they put it on your record? No Eddie Mr. Shivery said it's not going on my record. You know I asked him, what are my chances to go home next month? And he said as long as I don't try to hurt any staff member here it looks good. Why did he say that Larry? That's why I got sent here from Warwick; I threatened to hurt my house manager there for messing with me. Yo Larry, are you going to the dance next Saturday? I don't know Gregory I have to see how many stars I have. I am going to Middle Town with Mr. Shivery this Sunday. I love it when he takes me out. I get a chance to talk to the girls and walk around that little slow country town. The steaks there are the best and Jive five Mr. Shivery always buy me a steak when I go with him.

Mail call, Mr. Johnson do you have any mail for me? No Coldwell no mail today. Man I'll be glad when I go home. Yo, Larry, I know what you mean. Say man my hearing is a month after yours if I get a shot I'm coming to Harlem to see you. Okay Sap, you come and see me and I'll show you the town Sap, and then I'm going to see you in Buffalo, and Sap said that's a bet Larry.

Sap and I always talked about how we made money out in the streets before getting caught. I think Sap and I, was the only two guys on Wing 5 in there for getting money, the other guys were in there for things like sticking up stores, rape, and murder. We promise to hook up when we got out; and get rich together. All I wanted to do is make money when I get out; I'd like to be rich by the time I make 21 years old.

Larry, is the dance at Valhalla this Saturday? Yeah Sap it is. Well I'm looking to get me some pussy at the dance. Let me look at the board to see if I have enough stars to go to the dance because I want to meet me a fine sister. Sap asked me "yo, Larry do you have enough stars, yes I'm in. Eddie are you going to the dance Yes Larry I'm there. Greg are you going to the dance. No man, I don't have enough stars. Well, Sap I'm going to see you tomorrow, later Larry, later man."

Yo, Larry you heard them guys in wing 3 and 4 wants to strike in the mess hall. Yes Sap, I hear them loud and clear and man I hope they wait until after the dance. What do they want to strike about? I'm not sure Larry, but I heard some shit about better food. Sap, I'm not down for a strike right now, I'm about to go home to get rich, and I have to get out of here. Yeah man, I know but what are we going to do Larry, later for them we will stay cool and see what happens.

"Larry you know that crazy nigger Herm from Brooklyn is in Wing three. So what, if he knows you're not down with the strike he will surely come at you. Man later for that punk, I'm going to the dance because I need to be around some girls. Yo, man those guys were suppose to strike today but they chicken out. Well at least we get to go to the dance tomorrow Eddie."

Yo Eddie, did you see Sap slow grinding on a fast record at the dance. Man my man was getting down dipping on the song Cowboys and Girls. Yo, she was fine too. Yo Sap, yeah Larry what's up? Nothing Eddie just want to ask you did you get the girls name? Yeah I got it. Are you going to write to her? I'm not sure. Larry that bull dagger girl was going to kick your butt at the dance. Man you should have seen your face. Man I started to break her neck; she come telling me, I'm dancing too close with her girl. Me and the broad was getting along fine before that bull dagger came and scared the hell out of that fine girl, causing her to leave me alone.

Larry Coldwell come here, yes Mr. Smith, Mr. Shivery said he will see you tomorrow. Okay Mr. Smith. Yo Sap, you heard that? Yeah man, that should be your going home news. Larry don't

LARRY LUV

forget I'm coming to see you when I get out, ok Sap. Yo Larry, yeah Eddie what's up? Are you going to the yard? Yeah man how about you Sap. Yeah I'm going to.

Larry here come Herm. Man, later for that chump. Say man why you guys won't get down with the strike? Because I did not want to be down, nobody talking to you Larry. Well I'm talking to you chump; don't come over here asking us no questions like someone had to give your punk ass an answer. Nigger that's why I keep my foot in your stupid ass, you have a big mouth. In your dreams chump I don't like your chump Brooklyn ass, so why don't you buzz off, punk. Alright Coldwell and Herm let's break it up before I put you two in the hole. I'll see you later big mouth. Later for you chump. Man Larry I thought you were going to hit that chump right in front of Mr. Smith, no Eddie, I just wanted to set that chump straight. Man that punk is begging for someone to kick his ass. Come on Sap let's play paddle ball man. Say Eddie you played very good yesterday during paddle ball. Eddie, do you know what is for breakfast this morning? I heard pancakes. Yo, Sap, they got pancakes I'm coming to breakfast. Yo, Larry, you see how the Brooklyn nigger was looking at you in the mess hall? Yeah I saw him Sap, later for that asshole. Coldwell come down here. Ok, here I come Mr. Smith. Hey Mr. Shivery how's things? Fine Coldwell, well when am I going home? Larry you will be going home on June 28th, 1968. Yeah, thank you Mr. Shivery. Larry I'll call you a week before your birthday so that you can sign the papers, alright Mr. Shivery. Yo, Eddie, I'm going back to Harlem next month! Yeah, thank God. Yo man, today is May 20th my birthday. Damn, man it seems like yesterday when I was ten years old. Well I'm 16 years old and a man now, and I really must take care of T.C.B. when I get out.

I'll be glad to see my brother Kaye and all my family. Damn, I've been gone for almost two years. I wonder what the streets look like. I can't wait to see Pipes, she been my girl since first grade.

Lights out guys, see you later Sap. Goodnight Larry. Hey Larry, you think you're going to sleep tonight? No man I don't think so; I keep hearing that song "give me a ticket for an airplane I ain't got time for a fast train, lonely days are gone, I'm going home, you see my baby done wrote me a letter". Eddie what's up my man, nothing much. What did Mr. Shivery say about your hearing? He said I'm sixteen now so they have to let me go this time. So my man I will be hot on your tail out there. Cool my man. I'll see you in Harlem my brother Larry Love. Sap when you see Herm tell that punk I said kiss my ass on Christmas in front of Macy's window. Ha, ha, ha man I'm not going to say anything to that fool. He will be looking for someone to give him a good fight now that your history. Damn, man I'm out of here tomorrow. I wonder what's going on out there?

Coldwell let's go. I'm coming man. Sap, I'll see you later. Hope everything turns out alright for you my man. Hell Larry like they told Eddie, I'll be 16 in a few months and they got to let me go to. Cool I'll see you in Harlem when you come, you have my number and address right? right, yo, Larry get a piece of that nuke for me, sure Gregory. Yo Larry stay cool man okay Eddie. Yeah man, I'll see you in sweet Harlem, stay cool.

Coldwell here are your clothes, thank you Mr. Smith. As soon as I get home I'm going to A. J. Lester's on 125th street to get me some new clothes, my man Douglas will put me down on what to wear. Well Coldwell tomorrow you are to report to 10 Lafayette Street. There they will send you to a job interview and you will also meet your probation officer. Take care Coldwell, and try to stay out of trouble. Thank you Mr. Shivery for all your help, take care Coldwell. Yo, here I go. I can't wait to sit on the stoop early in the morning this Saturday and watch the block come alive. First the hot dog man will set up his stand on the corner of 8th avenue right in front of the drug store. Man those franks are real good! The grocery store will be getting sodas and beers from the trucks delivered. And the number runner man will come out to set up for the early working people that are going to work. The number writers sure could dress and they sure walked fly. Officer Joe takes his place on the corner of 8th avenue of the block. Officer Joe is white but he was a very nice cop, and always respected everyone in the neighborhood. In fact Joe was just as much apart of our neighborhood as the grocery store the drug store and the hot dog stand. Oh yes, the vegetable stand is setting up also. I remember when my brother Kaye, Dough, Tony, Robert and a bunch of us would run by and grab sweet potatoes and take them to the backyard and make up a grill and cook our sweet potatoes. We called them Mickies' and boy they were good. Hell we would stay in the backyard for hours playing all kinds of games. We would have so much fun; and the only girl hanging with us was Donna who is Tony and Robert's sister. After we would get tired of the backyard we would leave the block and go anywhere that we could make some money. Most of the time, we would go to Macy's or Gimbals and steal clothes or whatever we could get our hands on. I remember the first time I hit a cash register; boy I got a lot of money that day. We all knew back then that if you hit a cash register never waste your time on the one dollar bills and change; always go for the big bills and take it all when you hit it. We would go on a stealing spree from one store on 34th street to the next store. We would hit one store and go to the train station and rent a locker put our stuff in there and go to the next store. I remember when the Movie "The Children of the Damn" came out, the Black kid had a bad Duffle coat. I went right down to Macy's and stole me one just like his and Doug stole him one as well. My brother Kaye, Dough, Tony, Robert, Donna and I would go to Long Island stealing. Our poor mothers got to know the city from picking us up at all the precinct stations in the city and we were only 8 to 11 years old. We had one stealing game where we would go to every supermarket around until we found a cart full of grocery unattended. We would steal the whole cart and go to somebody's house and cook the food. Most times that would be Doug's house because his father was always at work and his mother Mrs. Tuti would be next door to Hattie Mae's mother's house. The only problem with going to Doug's house is that his big brother June Bug and his personal butt kisser one eye friend Puby would take most of our stuff. Doug's brother Ronald would be there also acting like he was with us when we stole the groceries. Ronald was our coach when we played basketball or baseball as children; he was about two years older than all of us and he thought he knew everything. One evening in the summer of 1963, we were all sitting on building 260, his stoop snapping on each other and someone slapped Ronald upside the head and he thought I did it. I told him that I didn't do it but he hit me anyway and the two of us started fighting hard. I beat him up that day and he told me I'm going to have to fight him again tomorrow. Whenever two guys from the block fought, everyone gets in the middle of the street stopping the cars from coming through the block so that the two fighters could get it on and have a fair fight where they could still be friends after the fight. Anyway I kicked Ronald's butt the next day as well, so he did not want any more after that.

Back in those days we would all stand on 8th avenue corner and rob all the kids who tried to pass our block to get to 125th street to shop. All the clothes stores were on 125th street and to get there from downtown you had to pass by 122nd street the best and tough block in Harlem. Yeah, I know all the blocks could make that claim, but our block has so many kids in it until they had to make it a play street; It was the first play street in Harlem and can't no other block make that claim. I remember when we first moved to 122nd street in 1960, from Spanish Harlem on 115st between 5th and Madison avenue before that we lived in Hell's kitchen on 60st street between 9th and 10th avenue in Manhattan. While living in Hell's kitchen there was a Catholic Church in the block and the

Nuns would give us lunch or something like that; one day the Nun gave me a bad egg which I ate not knowing better and I got sick to the point that I was taken to the hospital for food poisoning in 1958. Back then we had one of those real little TV's with a very thick glass on the screen in Hell's kitchen, and my brother Kaye went to turn the channel while we were eating one day and he had all this pig feet juice dripping off his hand when he touched the TV and he got the shock of his life. I took a broom stick and pushed him away from the TV; it happened in about 1958. My brother Kaye was always my main man. Kaye was the only guy I knew that was a better hustler than I was. To know Kaye was to like him a lot .

Here we are now living in 122nd street, and it was the best place in the world for me. We lived in building number 244 on the 3rd floor, apartment number 6. Right next to our building was building 260 and on the third floor, apartment 5 lived the Button family and our side windows was face to face and causing us to be friends and family neighbors. I remember my siblings and I were playing hide and see in our third floor apartment while my mother had gone out shopping. Well, I decided to hide from my sister Doris who was tagged it, by way of hanging out of the living room window which is in the front of our building as my hiding place to avoid being tagged your it. Everyone in the block thought I was going to jump. Someone told my mother about me hanging out the window when she came home and after my Iron cord butt whipping I never hung out the window again in my life. The first time I remember seeing the Button children my age was when I looked out our living room front window about the first week we moved in the block, which was in the summer. Well, one day in our first week living in 122nd St. I go to look out my front window and on my left I see these three children, two girls and one boy, in their underwear fighting over a baby bottle it was the damnedest thing I had ever seen because all three of them was around my age 8 years old, and I could not understand what in the hell were they doing fighting over who was going to suck that one baby bottle and why in the world they were only in their draws. That's the first time I had ever seen Pipes, Sandy and Curtis. The Button's windows and our windows were about five feet apart so we had no choice but to be close in some ways. In September I found myself in the same class as Pipes and she became my girl for the next 11 years. Pipes and I were feeling and kissing on each other from second grade until our 20s and whenever we got a chance too. Hanging out at Slims store across the street from my building was where all the kids on the block would be if you did not see them in the street. Bulldog Tarry also owned part of the joint Slim owned. Anyway we would be down their playing the juke box dancing, drinking sodas and eating potato chips. That's the first and only place I saw two couples doing the real dance called "doing the dog". It was Rachel and her brother Owen, and they were down on all fours humping their backs up in the air like cats does when they get ready to attack. I've never seen anyone do the dog like that again.

Next stop will be the Port Authority. Damn that was quick; it seems like I just got on this bus. I'll be glad to see my Mama sure hope she made me a coming home dinner. I'm going to see my probation officer as soon as I get to 42nd street. Okay, Coldwell; I'm Mr. Armstrong and I will be your probation officer for now. Here is an address for a job, its dishwashing see Mr. Taylor when you get there. I said to myself man, fuck that dishwashing job I am not a slave for no one. I took the information from him and headed up town on the fastest thing I knew to get me home which was that train Duke Ellington song about (take the A Train). One thing about riding the "A" train in those days was, that you got a chance to watch white people disappear; that is once the A train gets to 59th street all the white people would get off and the only people remaining on the train are those going up to Harlem and were African Americans that lived in Harlem. Well, here I go, just getting off the Train to walk down St. Nicholas Avenue to 122nd street because 123 street and St. Nicholas is like one third the length of a city block; it's a square; I would cross to 8th avenue which is about 20 feet from St. Nicholas avenue at 122nd Street, and then over to 8th avenue to my side of 8th avenue which is the uptown side and I am now back on my block.

CHAPTER 5

Knock, knock who is it? me Larry, Mommy; Larry is home. I can hear my mother still say "son trouble is easy to get into but hard to get out of." Hi Anne girl you sure have grown. Anne is my third sister from my father. I have eight sister's Elouise, Carolyn, Doris, Rosetta, Anne Deloris, Oranda, Veronica and Sandra. My oldest two sisters had the same father who molested my mother when she was a little girl. Her mother, Ma Dolly, made her sleep between her husband which lead to my mother giving birth to Elouise and my sister Carolyn. My younger sisters had different fathers. I also have four brothers Johnny Kaye, Gregory, James whom we call PeeNut and Haroldine who was born in 1969, and has a different father. Yo, Larry man you look good. What's up Kaye, it sure is good to see you my man. It's good to see you too Larry. Come on man let me take you over to Delores's house, everyone is hanging out up there. Hold on Kaye, let me see Mommy. Hi Mommy, hi son, how are you, I'm fine. "Tomorrow I'll give you some money to get some clothes", thank you Mommy. Ma I'll see you in a little while. Come on Larry, here I come Kaye. Delores lived across the street in building 257 on the top floor. When I went into Delores mother's living room, there was everyone in my age group there and it seem like most of them was hooked up as couples there. What really got me was there was my girl Pipes there in the arms of Charles. We called him "Foots" because his feet were so big. I was shocked to see my girl in his arms but I did not think much of it because I knew that Pipes was my girl no matter whose arms she was in. I also noticed this new guy name Steve who I had never seen before was hugged up on Delores real tight. Anyway, Kaye and Steve took me up to the roof and gave me a sniff of dope. The first time I ever tried it was when Mountain Dew soda first hit Harlem; I believe it was in 1964 or 1965, when I set up this robbery for Dough , Ronald who we called Airplane and Batman who is Robert. This kid was visiting Andy who lived in our block. Andy and I was hanging out in the block playing Lodes and his friend pulled out a big ten dollar bill to go buy something. Well, I told Dough and the rest about the money and they got the kid in the hallway and robbed him. I caught up with them on 121st street on the roof where they flew birds. When I asked for my cut they told me they spent all the money on two dollar bags of dope and if I wanted some I could have it. So, each one of them gave me a one on one sniff from each of their $2 bags. I did not like it at all and I never messed with it until this day after being away for about 2 years and on my first day home. I had no knowledge that Heroin was at such an epidemic proportion throughout Harlem as it was in 1968 when I came home from the Training school. Well, for some reason I accepted the sniff and after sniffing with Kaye we went to a house party. On our way to the party Pipes and Foots were walking together hand in hand and I was in the back of the crowd of about 20 youth. Well while at the party Pipes and I was slow grinding and I asked her, say Pipes I thought you were suppose to be my girl? And she said "I am Larry". So after the party Pipes and I were up front walking hand in hand and Foots was in back of us with his head down kicking a can. Everybody started sounding on him so hard about me taking my girl from him until one day he came at me and I had to kick his butt a few weeks later. Before I knew what hit me I was strung out on dope. I remember sniffing one day, skin popping the next, and mainlining the third day. I was home from a 2 years Training school stay. I could not figure out what in the hell happen to me. I was supposed to be getting paid and here I was with a drug habit. By August of 1968 I was selling drugs with this older guy who was about 30 years old and his name was John Slater. All I had to do was hold the dope and give the amounts of bags to whomever he told me to. One day we was sitting on the stoop when the police came all around us, John whispered to me "Larry are you clean?" and I whispered back to him, yeah man I'm clean. Well the police left and John asked me Larry where did you put the stuff? I told him I had it right in my pocket and John almost had a baby right on the spot. He said to me I thought you said you were clean, and I said to him I am; I took a bath last night. John said fool I meant are you clean with no drugs on you? That was the first time I had ever heard that phrase used before and the first time I ever sold drugs. Well John eventually went to jail a few weeks later and I did not know who his connect was. He did take me to pick up with him once over on 118 street and Park avenue in this Bar. One thing you never did was go up to the connect and ask him about drugs. If the connect did not come to you, you damn well better not go to him without being invited. They had this kid about 14 years old name Sickle selling drugs in the restaurant on 123rd street and 7th avenue on the uptown side of the street and he was making big money like $1,000 a day; I wanted to get in with him but I was hooked on them dam drugs. Anyway with John Slater in jail I was left with a three bags twice a day to the cooker habit and I had not been home two months yet. My man Sap, came to visit me in October 1968 and I was so strung out at the time till I was not good for my man and I knew I let him down. He had hundred dollar bills with him and was staying in a hotel downtown. We hung out for about two days and Sap went back to Buffalo and I never heard from him after that. Well Eddie Dixon came around my block a little after Sap. Eddie was strung out as well and he had a package of bundles that he was selling. We hung out together uptown on 142nd street and 7th avenue. We hung out at Slims Spot. Slim had the basement of this building on 141st and 142nd street and 7th avenue. Everybody that used dope would hang out in the boiler room where it was real dark and we would get high and go party in the next room. Eddie and I hung out for about six months. Our addiction got worst to the point that we stopped hanging with each other. The last time I saw him he told me his new name was Candy Land and that he was a stick up kid. One morning in August of 1968, at about 10am I was sitting on my stoop when Omar and Slim told me they were going to this girl's house name Zaytuna and asked me did I want to come. Omar used to be a part of my old gang before I went away. His brother Zadike and Rahiem his brother Lil Arkbar, Harmeen his brother Reggie and sometimes Bit and I would go downtown around Time Square and Grand Central Station and snatch rolls of quarters or dimes from the news stand. Back in the days they would leave all their change out where you could grab it. We also would send two guys into a store to act like they were going to steal something or have a fight and when the person at the cash register would leave the register for half a second to address the guys, one of us would ring up the register and only go for the 20's, 10's or 5 dollar bills. Well, Omar and Slim invited me to go with them, and we went to her house in building 238th in the block on the second floor across the hall from the number hall where we played numbers. When I saw Zaytuna, boy, she was as fine as Georgia wine and twice as nice. I had never noticed her in the block before. I later learned that she lived down south in Winston Salem North Carolina, and that every summer she and her younger sister came up to New York to stay with her mother who had moved into the block while I was in the Reform School. Zaytuna's sister was about five years younger than she was. So here's this fine 16 year old country girl and Hantiria who was just as fine as Zaytuna, the only thing is Hantiria and I grew up on the block together. Well the five of us are sitting around in Zaytuna's mother's living room jive talking. So I asked Zaytuna to put some music on. Well as faith would have it she played one of Smokey's old songs and she and I started grinding. I started whispering in her ear and kissing her. I told her lets go in the back room, and she said no; but that I could take Hantiria back there and so being the dog I was, I started moving in on Hantiria. Hantiria was very fine and just as hot. It seemed like all her hormones were kicking in at the same time. She had shoulder length hair and a waist so small all you wanted to do was hold on to it and her breasts stood up like head lights on a 57 Chevy. I don't know what happened to my two homeboys but at some point they left the apartment. When I realized it, I was alone with these two fine young girls. Like I said, I started moving in on Hantiria and she was all for my every move. Zaytuna said she was going downstairs for a while and that the two of us could use the living room. Well, the next thing I know is that Zaytuna comes running into the apartment telling Hantiria and I that her mother was coming up the block right now and that the two of us had to stop. I don't know about Hantiria but I was like a fighter jet taking off on an air craft carrier once you get to the point of no return there's nothing you can do but take off or fall head long into the ocean destroying a millions of dollars aircraft. I was not about to do something as shameful as that; so I said to myself the hell with her mother and my promise to Hantiria. I took off for the blue skies and like a jet I shout out 100% pure 16 year old protein. Hantiria and I had our moments many times after that day, but the funniest thing of all is that from that day on Zaytuna was my girl. I remember when I was about 12 years old Pop Corn Mary lived across the street from my building and every time she wanted to hold my bike she would have to agree to meet me behind the staircase in her building in the basement where the two of us would be kissing and rubbing on each other for what seem like hours. Well, Zatuna and I get together was different from Pipes and me. Pipes never knew anything about Zaytuna because Zaytuna never hung out with us on the block. One day Zaytuna got sick and was in Mount Sinai Hospital. I would go visit her and found out she had an operation. It was a small one I don't remember what for. One day while visiting her, this older lady was visiting her and praying over her. So I waited until the lady was done and left then I asked her did she believe in that garbage and she said yes, so I left it at that. I never believed in any of the God concept at that time, in spite of the fact that my siblings and I was brought up in Saint Andrew's Baptist Church. That was a time in Harlem when all the church preachers drove nice big black Cadillac cars; and we would call them slick hustlers pimping the people. Kaye and I was considered two of the bad kids in the block but we had to go to church on Sundays and dress up in suits on Easter for church when none of our friends in the block went to church at all. Well by the end of the summer of 1968 I was strung out on drugs and everyone that was at Delores house that day Kaye brought me up there were strong out on heroin as well. Zaytuna never knew I was using drugs and I would never let her see me under the influence of heroin. In September of 1968 Zaytuna went back down south to school. I don't know how I got caught out there because I never liked using dope nor how it made you feel or act. Nonetheless here I was strong out on heroin at 16 years old. I wish the Annex State Training School would have said something about the wide spread heroin epidemic that hit New York City from 1965-1968, before they let me out at least that way it would not have been able to blind side me the way it did, remember I came home to get rich not to be someone's 16 year old junkie. There were lots of things happening there in Harlem and throughout the country. The Temptations had us doing fine on Cloud Nine and the Black Panther Party had their East Coast office on 122nd street and 7th avenue. They would try to recruit us every day; also Joanne Chisholm was on St. Nickalas avenue in the warehouse on 123rd Street across from where Kaye and I sold water melons when we were kids. The only time we listen to them was when we were high and wanted to get out of the cold, so we would sit in their place acting like we were listening. I remember the snow blizzard of 1969 and I was so strung out on that dope with no money; I went out to make a sting by the time I got to 125th street and St. Nicholas avenue train station I looked like the snowman, I went back home and my poor Mother seen me come in the house looking so sad till she gave me ten dollars of which I used the money to cop some dope. The summer of 1969 came and Stevie Wonder's "My Cherie Amour" was playing in every record store along with Louis Armstrong playing. For some reason 1969 seemed to be the last year of my innocence. When Zaytuna came up that Summer I made sure she did not see me all strung out on dope. I would notice her coming my way from a good six to seven cars away and go into the nearest building to wait for her to go by. I know she was confused and wanted to know what was going on with me, but I was too ashamed of what I had become to let her see old lover boy messed up like that. I was strung out on drugs for about two years and in those two years I did a 9 month bid on Riker's Island and a 6 month bid for burglaries on stores. That was my hustle when I was strung out on that damn dope; I would break into stores for clothes, liquor and cigarettes. Those items were very easy to sell and there was always a need for them in my Harlem. The only thing and time of my life that I was a failure at was being a junkie; I made a bad junkie. After doing 4 ½ months on Riker's Island out of a 6 month sentence for burglary I made up my mind that I once again was going to get rich. I promised myself that I did not want to ever use dope again. So when I got out in 1970, from Riker's Island a lot of the guys from the block was in the drug program on 123rd street called ARC. Steve, Blood, Jay, Michael Martin, and a few other guys was in the program, so I started hanging out there along with some of the guys we met there. My brother Kaye never stopped using heroin when most of the guys from 122nd street stopped. ARC would feed us and throw a party every Friday at the program. They had some fine girls in the program as well. One thing that always hurt me was that most of the guys on drugs in my block got their lives together at the program but for some reason none of our girls that hung out with us got off the drugs during the 1970s; there was Pipes, Debra, Delores, Christian, Vanessa Brown and Yvonne Brown, Hantira and many others. It would be years later before some of the girls got themselves together. It was sad because throughout Harlem after the assassination of Reverend Doctor Martin Luther King Jr. in April of 1968, the Harlem community and all major inner cities were flooded with dope and all other kinds of drugs.

There was dope being sold on just about every corner block in Harlem, and they had us believe that it was the Mafia who was responsible for the drugs flooding America. But I now come to believe it was the same people that have these drugs flooding America today, and it sure is not the Mafia. Well here we were a lot of young men no longer using drugs and did not want to work for the white man or have anything to do with him because he is so unfair to us and abusive to minorities; so as long as the white man gave us Harlem we stayed as far away from him as we could. Our average space was within a 10 block radius of our communities. The next thing I know is that names like Gold Finger, Wytusie, Fat Jack, Stick Man, and Nicky Bonds started ringing throughout Harlem. Somehow I got the news that my man Eddie Dickson who we now called Candy Land had been killed. He was shot by the police while sticking up a token booth in Harlem. Then I heard that my hustling partner when I was a kid got shot, my man Bit was sticking up a token booth clerk and got shot in the back by the police that year also. In 1970 the police was shooting stick up kids rather than arresting them. Bit did not die but he walked with a limp in his left leg for the rest of his life and to this very date.

Then Nooky from 121St got shot and killed by the cops. Nooky was from 121st street and he hung out on our block. Nooky was real nice with his hands and he had the heart of a gun fighter. Nooky, his brother Dirty Al, Price, Teddy and some other guys would go into a Bar and rob the joint with nothing but a crowbar which they only used to break into the jukebox. All of them were strung out on dope and that was how they made their money to get high. The police knew that they never used a gun, but because they were robbing Bars in Harlem for the past two years, one day after they had robbed this Bar uptown the police followed them back to 122nd street between 7th and Lennox Avenue and jumped out on them and shot them up. They killed Nooky and shot Teddy in the arm. Teddy and Dirty Al got caught and went upstate for years. Well Zaytuna did not come up for the summer of 1970, and I started selling Reefer for my brother in law **Henry**, because I did not want to work for the system, where there was no real opportunities for uneducated young Black men that I was able to see. All we as young Black uneducated males had to look forward to was the street life which was just fine with me. As I built my Reefer clientele up I was selling three and five dollar bags of smoke. I also went back to smoking Reefer. My Crew and I would do everything with smoke you could imagine. We would boil it and drink it like you drink tea and also eat it. I remember one $3 bag of smoke I had gave me 10 joints out of it. My Reefer smoking, Crew was Charlie B his real name is Tony White and Bulldog, who came from 119th street and St. Nicholas avenue. One day in 1970, Tony and I brought him into 122nd street and he never left it. Our block had that kind of impact on people. We had everything going on in our block. The numbers man would come out of the number hole at 3pm with the first number and make a sign, once he came out you would hear old ladies sucking their teeth or stomping their feet; and if you did not know the signs you would think all these old women had gone mad at the same moment. The number man would walk to the corner with one fist in the air that meant an 0 came out or he would pat his head which meant a 9. Sometimes he would say something like "the dead is out" and that meant all three numbers for the dead were 679; then you would look and see about 3 to 12 guys standing around shooting dice, and the house man cutting the game. To be the house man all you have to do is have a few sets of dice, take some chalk and draw two lines one on the left side and one on the right side with each line about 5 feet long and 4 feet wide, then you connect both lines across with the gutter curb as your headboard then start playing with the dice and before you knew it someone would come up and want to either shoot them or bet you lose. I've seen and have been in games that start off betting for nickels and dimes and end up betting for hundreds of dollars. The houseman controls the crap game, by making sure no one tries to put loaded dice in the game, he also holds the main bet. When a guy shoots the dice he would put up one dollar, then the houseman must get his bet on; he says to whoever is around the crap game "the shooter shoots one dollar can he get a fader", the fader is the one who bets against the shooter, the fader will say something like "I'll fade the nigger, let the nigger shoot". The houseman will then get the faders dollar and tell the shooter to shoot. The houseman must make sure he gets the faders money before he tells the shooter to shoot because the house is responsible for that bet no matter how small or big. All betters must stand on the outside of the chalk line. A good house man will always make sure the crap game is right under a street light because the game almost always run into the late hours of the night. He would also have a brown shopping bag with him. The houseman stands at the head of the box he has drawn on top of the curb with his shopping bag between his legs to cut the game. The house cuts like this, the shooter starts off shooting one dollar, he either throw 7 or 11; after he throws a number and before 7 comes up he hits his number, then the house will get the two dollar on. The shooter could either, take the two dollars and pass the dice or he could let it ride. Always the shooter will let it ride, so the house gets the 2 dollars on; and the shooter hits 7; well now the shooter has 4 dollars with the same options as before the shooter let it ride. Once again he either hit 7 or 11 on the first roll or he hits a number before crapping out. He then has 8 dollars that he lets ride. So the house now cuts the third pass and every pass after that from the shooter as he continues to shoot the dice from this time up until he loses or takes his money and pass the dice. So then instead of shooting 8 dollars, the house cut one dollar which leaves the 8 dollar shooter only shooting 7 dollars. The house can only cut one dollar at a time no matter how high the pot is. Then you have the side bets going on. Some gamblers specialize in side bets. They call it the fast field. They would either have it written on a card board or a piece of cloth or they would write it on the ground in front of them. The fast field would go something like this. They bet the shooter never makes a number in his whole life; bet he don't 6/9 bet he don't 10/11 bet he don't 5/8 or 10/4. These numbers are the numbers that the fast field bets the shooter will not make before he 7 out after he has a number to make and they always give you odds on these numbers like if you put 3 dollars on 6 or 9 and either one of those two numbers come up before the shooter sevens out then you get your 3 dollars and the fast fields 5 dollars. The best thing I liked about a dice game is the many jokes and jive talk that the shooter and better say to each other. This guy name Lorenzo lived on our block and he was real cool. I don't know where he came from he was another one of so many who fell in love with 122nd Street. Anyway Lorenzo had a gold tooth in the front of his mouth with a process hair style. If you would say something like, hey Lo give me five dollars and Lorenzo would say something like "I won't give a cripple crab a crutch if I owned a lumber yard", are you'd hear "nigger get it like Grant got Richmond". And the shooter would say "come on baby need a new pair of shoes, and I make this number for bread and meat the days I don't hit is the days I don't eat". The dice language is real slick. The last responsibility of the houseman is to give a shooter their house when the shooter gets broke. The house that he gets is enough cab fare to get his broke tail away from the crap game standing around looking sad because he lost his rent money and can't go home to his wife and kids broke; so he just stands there swallowing bets. Old man Freddy Pounder ran most of the big money dice games on 122nd Street. A few buildings down you would have the young mothers in their mid to late teens playing Pity Pat card game for quarters. Most times it would be, Bub Strub sister from building 236. She was fine and she is the only girl I ever really liked who was born and raised on 122nd street. She was coco brown with shoulder length hair and had a fine built. Her daughter by her and Randy became my god-daughter and we called her Mamay. Then there's Pam, who lives in my building with Miss Ola May on the first floor. We used to go for cousins. Pam was dark skin with fair hair, and was about 5 feet tall and was built like a brick house. **Tammy** was Mrs. Wynn's granddaughter. Mr. Wynn sold the bootleg liquor when the stores closed at midnight. His liquor was so weak until you had to drink half the bottle to feel it. Tammy was your average looking sister and big boned. Tammy and Peaches had the same father but not the same mother. Then there was my sister Anne who was my third sister from my father's side. She was dark skin with a round oval face, short hair, big chest and fair skin. These girls could play some Pity Pat. Pity Pat is a card game the first one with three pairs win. You get five cards and must pluck the 6th card to make three pairs, the first one to do so win's the hand. They also bet on the highest spade on the side, and more than likely my mother would be selling home cooked dinners there to them. Everybody in the block loved my mother's cooking especially her bread pudding. All the time our mother's would be sitting on the stoop gossiping and trying to figure out what the next number would be. You would look up at the window of any building and there would be a window raising grandmother yelling at a kid to come upstairs. Most of 122nd street actions was near 8th avenue. My building is about 3 buildings from 8th avenue which put me right in the mix of everything. Anyway when Bulldog or anyone outside of 122nd street saw all that action and care we had for each other they would almost always claim 122nd street as their block. Another thing about 122nd street is that you could not do anything to anyone on that block if you did not live on it. I remember one day these two guys are walking through 122nd street with a TV. One guy was carrying a TV he had on this dirty green shirt and brown pants with cigarette burns on the legs his sneakers was so old that they was past his age of 21. His partner was wearing a dirty black tee shirt that once was white with jeans that stood up by themselves, once you take them off and with a pair of run down shoes. It was clear that these guys were not from our block. So I said "Yo, where are you going with that TV"? The little chump with the TV said none of your business and kept walking toward 8th avenue. Now mind you this is in the summer time around 4pm when all the guys are out. So I said to the guys they can't leave the block until I check with the people in the block that their apartments are clear. Well needless to say the two chumps tried to step to me; so I gave the order to my boys to not let them move. My Crew then surrounded them; you had Charlie B, Bulldog, Ray Day, Bubby, Steve, Al and about 12 more guys around these two guys. I took this old RCA 19inch black and white screen TV from them. That TV was heavy it must have weighed about 60 pounds. Come to find out the TV belonged to Miss Smith a little old lady that lived by herself in a one bedroom apartment in building 226 near 7th avenue. Once we discovered who the TV belonged to, I sentenced the two TV thieves to pain. The thieves were thrown down the basement of 261 building, the basement had about 12 steps to it, and once you're in the basement there's no other way out because the basement door is locked. So here we are looking down at these two chumps and their looking up at us with the look of mercy in their eyes. And with eyes of madness we begin to carry out the sentence of pain. Everyone started picking up soda bottles, wine bottles, beer bottles and bricks. We then started to stone them for the next five to ten minutes; and I don't know what ever happened to them after that, but what I do know is that I never saw them in 122nd street again. Togetherness was another reason why people from other blocks always claimed 122nd street. The main hangout spot was on the corner of 8th avenue in front of the fish and chip joint. Little Shorty owned the joint and he let me use it for my headquarters. When my brother Kaye and I were kids we use to sell watermelons for Shorty. Shorty had a red Chevy pickup truck. We would meet at the watermelon spot on 123rd and St Nicolas Avenue where the 28th precinct is now located, early in the morning during the summer days to hire ourselves out to the truck owners. My brother and I would always make sure we worked together. We got paid $5 dollars for about 6 hours and all the tips we made. Our job was to carry the melons to people cars, stoop or to their apartments. It was not easy carrying a 12-15 pound melon up 5 flights of stairs and to only receive a nickel tip. We would curse that tipper all day as a cheap mother hub bur and a stingy nigger until the next stingy tipper comes along. Shorty and I go back to the days when I was 8, 9 and 10 years old. There were often funny and strange incidents taking place in 122nd Street. I remember one Sunday morning in 1971 this man and lady came running through the block. The guys and I was sitting on the stoop at my building, jive talking when a car comes screaming after these two. The next thing you know is that they are shooting at each other. I saw the lady get her head shot off, the car then speeds off; and when the smoke was clear we went over to check out what just happened. When we get to building 263 we saw that it was the lady's wig that was shot off her head; the lady and her man were shot but still on their feet and trying to get out of the block. During the summer of 1971 Gold Finger and Watusi names was ringing loud bells in the underworld of the drug game. Well as the drug game picked up in Harlem this guy called Stick Man, was one of the smoothest guys in the game. He was a real fly guy from the eastside of Harlem and it seemed like out of nowhere, everyone started selling drugs. Stick Man was a slim good looking dude with a nice basketball game. They say that a NBA team came to Harlem to offer Stick Man a contract. It was said that they offered him $100,000 dollars a year to play in the NBA, and that Stick Man took the guy with the offer for a ride in his Rolls Royce and picked up $100,000 dollars from his dealers. He then said to the agent here I make that kind of money in a day. Stick Man was so cool that he would come to the Pro Rucker where the top street ball players and NBA pro players came to play in the summer time. He would come to the Rucker on 155th street and 8th avenue on the uptown side of the street from the Polo Grounds. The games were on Sundays, and the street ball players would put on a show equal and sometimes surpassing the show one gets from the NBA. Here comes Stick Man with two of the finest sisters in Harlem. He would sit down and put his legs out and the two honeys would take off his alligator shoes and put on his Spaulding sneakers and tie them for him. All the real good basketball players wore Spaulding sneakers in those days. Stick Man would have his mink coat on at night standing in front of The Shadow Mar Bar on 123rd street and 7th avenue uptown side of the street. The Shadow Mar Bar was one of the bars where a lot of the young up and coming big time drug dealers hung out at, and across the avenue on the downtown side of 7th avenue between 123rd and 124th street was the Plus Two Bar where Watosi and the older drug dealers hung out at. They all got along with each other as they respected the street rules that govern the drug dealing game. I missed my Zaytuna and every now and then the thought of her would pop up in my mind and when I got smoked up, I would stand on the stoop of 263 which is across from 238 where her mother lived on the second floor front window. I would look up at her window and imagine seeing her there looking out at me. Our song was "Just my Imagination" by the Temptations; especially the part that said "each day through my window I watch her as she passes by, I say to myself your such a lucky guy to have a girl like her is truly a dream come true." Zaytuna would be standing at the window looking finer than Cleopatra the queen of the Nile in my mind. Bulldog, Charlie Bee, Bubby, Michael Martin and I made up the most part of my crew. We would go to 117th street and Manhattan Avenue to buy our Reefer. There were several groups of guys out there selling it. A guy name Little Larry on 117th street who we always looked to cop from first, because his Cheebah was always at top quality. Little Larry was about 5 feet 5 inches and real light skin like Thurgood Marshall with curly hair. He was never a dresser; the clothes he wore were like taxi cab driver cloths. In fact he was a cab driver and a reefer dealer. Larry liked me and Bulldog, and he would either give us extra bags of smoke or take short money from us with no problem. The smoke on 117th street was sold for $5 dollars a bag. You also had 9 Finger John, who sold Reefer from his first floor apartment on Manhattan avenue corner. John was light skin like little Larry and about Larry's age. Both of them appear to be in their early thirties, and then you had the young guys our age selling smoke. One of these groups was on 117th street corner building off Manhattan avenue in the block. They were Moody, Hollis and Pop as well as a few other guys. We would buy from them when we could not catch up with Lil Larry or 9 Finger John. Then you had the 8th avenue of 117th street dealers. They were Mace, William, Otis, Little Boo, Tyrone and others. The problem with buying from the guys our age was that they would try to look down on us. No matter how many bags of smoke we brought; and they would never give us an extra bag or take a short from us. A short is like wanting to buy 6 bags at $5 dollars a bag but you only have $26.75. The younger guys hated to take a short. So we looked for our main man Little Larry who never had a problem with our short money. Once my crew and I copped our smoke we would go around to 117th street and St. Nicholas avenue next to the Catholic School where there was an abandoned building. There was a rail there to the building where we would sit on and roll up our smoke; this block only had one building with people living in it and half of that building was abandoned. Across the street from our smoke building was the side of the Wilthon Hotel and a disco that we called the Cave. The hotel took up 80 percent of the side of the street. Then there was a record shop that seemed to play music just for us. On the corner of 117th street and St. Nicholas avenue was a housing building that had middle income working families living there. This building had a bunch of fine girls that hung out on the stoop. These girls would be watching us as we smoked and acted crazy. So one day I went over to rap to them. I was smoking a joint and when it reached the roach stage I threw it on the ground at about the time I approached the group of girls. When two of them broke wild, and almost knocked each other down, as well as knock me down trying to get that roach. Well, that's how we met Jonda her sister Jacky, Fat Bee, Wonita and Josilin her sister. From that day on Jonda and her girls started hanging out on 122nd street. They not only fell in love with 122nd street, but also started dating some of the guys on my block. Jonda and I was supposed to hook up but it never happened because one day I saw Jonda dressed in a white blouse and it was button up wrong and the collar of the neck was greasy black and she was walking eating a piece of fried chicken and that turned me all the way off from wanting to hook up with her. Jonda was not fine but she was pretty. She was coffee brown with hair reasonably long and strong built. To see her at 18 years old, you would want to get with her without a doubt. Yes she was far from my South Carolina college girl Zaytuna. One day Jonda attacked me, once by kicking me up my butt when I walked away from her in the after school night Center at PS 144, and mind you, to touch me in any way was in clear violation of the by-laws of one of the baddest guys on 122nd St. However I let her slide that time because I don't like fighting girls because as a child I used to see my mother and father fighting each other as if they were strangers in a bar. In those days adult couples would be fighting with knives, chairs, bats and even Lye. Yes in the late fifties and early sixties a can of Lye held the same respect as a foolish knuckle head with a gun in his or her hands today. One of the fight watchers would yell out, "look out she got Lye" and the whole crowd would haul tail getting out of the way from that person with the Lye in their hand. It seem like only the women would use Lye in a fight. Lye was purchased from the grocery store for about 10 cents a can. It was used to clean grease from pots and skillets. In those days I never really seen anyone get Lye thrown on them; but it was always a good threat to use on a person to get them to back up off you. You would say something like "I bet I'll wash your ass in Lye or I'll put that hot shit on your tail, if you don't leave me alone." I know this guy from 121st street name Jim Booty he slapped this lady; as the story was told, and she came back and caught him on 8th Avenue next to Singleton Bar and called him by his name as his back was to her and when he turned to answer her with an onslaught of bitches coursing words. As the story is told she had a pot of Lye in her hand and when he turned to curse her she dashed it in his mouth and face. It's said that he took off running and howling with his face; dropping off him. I did see Jim Booty sometime later and it was clear to all that he was hit with Lye; his face and hands were messed up. I don't know what ever happened to the lady. But Jim Booty never slapped anyone after that as I know of. By the way it's an art to making a good effective pot of Lye. It can be made with syrup, coca cola or water. If you don't know what you're doing you can very easily become your own victim messing with Lye. So

I did not like fighting girls because of my mother and father fights. Well the second time Jonda and I had it out was when she called me a faggot, some months after getting away with kicking me in the butt when we was in the after school center at PS 144. At this time we all were in Singleton Bar on 122nd Street and 8th Avenue drinking and selling drugs. Well it was time to put an end to Jonda's out right disrespect to the baddest guy on 122nd street. When we were kids no one was allowed to call the other faggot or nigger without a fight. But now it was cool to say "my nigger, if you don't get no bigger". Well it was now time to teach Jonda a lesson, So I hit her a couple times with my fist and she got the message loud and clear that you don't mess with that crazy fool Love god. Again as a kid in Harlem calling someone faggot or a nigger was like declaring war with them. The Black Panthers are the ones who helped us to accept being Black as well as James Brown song "Say it loud, I'm Black and I'm proud", and also Malcom X; as he taught us to stand strong and tall as a Black Man. On the corner of my block on 7th Avenue was the Black Panthers East Coast Headquarters. And the Panthers would be trying to get us to join them. However, all we wanted to do is make money. They would offer us rifles and guns if we joined them, but all we wanted was to make money and have fun. What we did take from the Panthers, is the idea of staying out of the system. So, not one of us out of about 35 guys between the ages of 16 through 21 wanted anything to do with a 9-5 job, which there was only a few jobs that we knew of and they were jobs in the garment district around 33 street, and no promise of any financial success at the time. But there was so much money to be made in the streets that we could see and touch to believe that one can achieve it. In 1971 everyone started selling drugs I was in and out of the drug game since 1968 selling. In 1971, it was time for me to take a big step up. I started selling dime capsules of cocaine on 116th street between 7th and Lenox Avenue. Homeboy Duke brought me in; along with Michael Martin who was about 5 feet 6 inches tall and had a real bad cockeye. Mike always had a girl or two in spite of his cockeye. He was still a good looking brother and Terry was known as Showboat, and he was down with us. Terry was cool and scared as hell to sell drugs. Yet it was so easy until a scared guy had just enough heart to make money. We hustled right in front of Fat Jack's restaurant which was on the side of 116th street where the traffic is going east, about four doors up from the bar Jim Daniel which is three doors up from the Mosque #7. I remember one day this white guy was buying some coke from someone on the block. There was about a good 30 guys and girls selling on that block, and most of them were from Greensboro, South Carolina. Our gang was the only New Yorkers on the block. Anyway this guy passes the white guy the drugs in front of the Mosque and a Muslim brother saw it. Everyone on the block knew not to sell around the Mosque. So the Muslim see's the sale going down and he thinks the white guy is selling drugs to the black guy. So he steps to the white guy and starts yelling at him about selling drugs to blacks. The poor white guy got scared and took off running up 116th to 7th avenue. By this time four Muslim brothers has gathered and ran after the white guy. They caught the guy in the middle of the block and beat the hell out of him. They let him go after the butt kicking.

Marvin Gaye's "What's Going On" played at the record shop across from where we hustled. Black Pearl was one of the finest sister's on the block; and she was also just as tough as everyone else on the block. Black Pearl was as dark as a sweet quiet night standing about 5 feet 8 inches taller than life when she wore boots. Her face was filled with beauty in spite of the wig which she wore well. She was the only girl on 116th street who shot dice with the guys in the street. When it came her turn to shoot the dice, she would back that big soul sister butt up in the air with leather pants on and talk just as much dice jive talk then any guy playing. She was a country girl from South Carolina that was a fine walking gold mine; she could make money. Her man was in jail he got busted with a key of cocaine. She waited loyally for him to come home. I was selling dime capsules of cocaine like crazy, and I had all kinds of customers. I had one blind guy who always brought 40 dimes when he came and my man was in a wheelchair spending $400 every other day. When Michael, Showboat, Duke and I first started out our goal was to fill up this golf bag that was empty with the money we made from selling the drugs. Well the bag became 2/3rd filled after about 2 months of work. I was working through the summer of 1971 like crazy till I did not realize that my beloved Zaytuna, had once again not come up for the summer. We got along good with the country boys on 116th street, and we all looked out for each other. One Friday night a bunch of us young dealers was in old man Hank's variety store around 8pm playing the picker low and cooling out, when the cops that was portrayed in French Connection movie came into 116th street drunk and crazy. They raided the variety store and took about 12 of us guys and girls out in hand cuffs for nothing. By the time we got to the 28th precinct on 123rd street between 8th and 7th avenue all the old ladies on 116th street was there in the precinct raising hell about Popeye raiding the block and taking us children to jail for no reason. Well the mothers of 116th street raised so much hell until they let all of us go from the precinct within hours of arriving there. One thing about 116th street was, don't let a stickup kid come on 116th street for he is just about guaranteed not to make it out alive. It does not matter how many they are or how armed they might be. One day the block started chasing a stickup kid that ran smack into a city MTA bus traveling east. It was said that the guy got killed when he hit the front bus window. Well by the end of the summer of 1971, I looked into our golf bag and it was empty. I asked Duck "what happened to the money?" He said something that did not make sense about the money. Then I learned that while Michael, Showboat and I are in Castle Hill, in the Bronx sleeping, Duke was out partying and gambling and losing all the money. Well, it was time for me to move on. Duke did not like that because I was the one doing the most selling in the gang and as a result our breakup was very ugly. Here I was back on 122nd street by October of 71 and there was a light Heroin panic. The panic left the streets with almost no drugs on the street. In 122nd street we sold $2 duce bags which came 15 bags to a 15 bag bundle was called a half of a load and a load was 30 bags. Almost always you got a half of load. When a guy got a package on the lowest level of the drug game; it was $2 bags of drugs in half loads of 15-100 loads. In 122nd street we had about 10 guys that sold bundles and there was room enough for all of us to get paid; everyone in our block got money. I was selling about 25 bundle bags a day. A bundle of 15 $2 dollar bags came to $30 dollars a bundle. The dealer gets $10 dollars and the boss gets $20 dollars and the boss does not want his $20 short one penny. I would come out by 8am and set up shop on the block. The first thing I would do is checkout the block and roof tops for cops, stick up kids, and stash stealers. Once the coast was clear I would then stash the bigger part of my package somewhere on the block, be it in someone's apartment with their approval or in an abandon building. Then I would take about 5 bundles with me in a pouch or something that allows me to get rid of them all at once if the police run up on me. The key to selling drugs back in the days was to know your customers by face are to know what any drug customer looks like; and you must know the language of the drug game. There is clearly an art to selling drugs, and if you're not talented in the game of drug dealing you're sure to go to jail for a very long time for a direct drug sale. When I come out early in the morning, I would try to sell about 50 bundles by 10am; because after 10am all the rest of the guys start coming out to sell their drugs as well. Almost all of us got our drugs from the same guy. We all grew up looking up to him. He lived next to the Chinese restaurant on 8th avenue between 122nd and 121st street. Blue was a very cool guy. He drove a Mustang and always looked out for us. That was Airplane's main man. Plane was selling drugs for Blue since he was about 16 years old, Airplane's real name is Ronald Mabry. He lived in 260 next to my building. His brother was Douglas who we called Doug. Doug was my best friend on the block, and he was the youngest wino I've ever known. At about 9 years old we had to pull Doug out of the basement on 8th avenue next door to Mr. and Mrs. Greens hardware store on 8th avenue. Doug was not a drug dealer because he would use dope too much to sell it. Out of all my brothers Kaye, Greg and Peanut, I was the only one dealing. My brothers got caught up in using drugs as well. I averaged about 25 bundle sales a day. We would sell our drugs until about 6pm then take a break and go see the latest movie on 42nd street and Broadway; when it only cost $10 cab ride from 122nd St. to 42nd St. 122nd street had not officially become mine yet. However, I started claiming it as mine around this time. On 116th street to 114th street from 7th Avenue to Manhattan Avenue everyone that hustled drugs there sold $75 quarters. A quarter consisted of a full quarter serving spoon of scrambled dope. This is dope that has been cut with quinine and lactose. Only a few people knew how to cut dope real good and the right way without messing up the package. A good cut man was looked up to as a brilliant chemist that everyone in the drug game would want to have on their team. The guy's downtown was making big money. They were getting their quarters for $30 apiece and selling them for $75 dollars apiece. Everybody in Harlem from 145th street down to 112th street was making money hand over fist in 1971. Sly Stone came out with "It's a Family Affair" and we claimed it as our song for 122nd street. Every Wednesday night we would go to the Apollo Theater, Wednesday was when the acts changed. We would see the shows before the actors got caught up in the New York scene. Wednesday was the first act and you also got the amateur show. We had so much fun at the Apollo on Wednesdays. Well back on the block we started coming down hard on the junkies for some reason. And before you knew it, all the black customers would not buy from us. There was one thing about a junkie back then, and that is they are not going to allow you to treat them bad. No matter how good your dope is a junkie will only let you talk to him but so bad a few times. After that he would walk 20 miles to buy some garbage rather than spend a dime with you. Anyway there were enough white customers pulling up on the block that everyone selling on 122nd street made money. Zaytuna came up for the summer of 72, she was looking finer then ever. And her love for me was still very strong. She began to invite me to go back to Winston Salem, North Carolina with her. She promised to get me in school at A & T where she went; Zaytuna begged me to leave Harlem and go south with her. But I had no plans to leave my beloved 122nd street. Her mother hated my guts, she thought Zaytuna was too good for me; and that I was nothing but one of those ghetto niggers that would never amount to anything. I did not understand why her mother had such negative feelings about me then, but I can see it and understand it clearly today if my daughter would bring a Larry Love god child into my home back then.

CHAPTER 6

I also had a friend name Jim Danny who went to college in Miami in 1972. When he came home on school break he would offer me an opportunity to go to college with him. Zaytuna and JD's offer to me for going to college was good, it's just that they believed in me when I did not believe I could handle the college experience and with my thinking at the time it is no way in the hell I could have handled being in college. In 1972, the Black Panthers had the police on the run for real. The cops were scared to get out of their police cars. It looked like every week a cop was either getting killed or shot up. The reason the police were targeted by the Black Panthers is because Law Enforcement represents the right hand of the political system that was issuing oppressive orders upon our society and the only way to reach them was by way of the connection to those that make these oppressive rules and those who enforces them. The Panthers were not against white people in general because there were many white people in support of the Black Panther Movement. The Black Panthers were fighting the hands of oppression that continues to oppress low income communities to this day. We have former Panther members like *Dr. Matula Sicoure, and Durubba Moore* who has been in the Jim Crow prison system for over 30 years for acts of liberation and not criminality behavior. They are political prisoners deserving of freedom from incarceration after serving over 30 years of incarceration.

    The Heroin panic of 72 did not last long and it seemed that after it was over everybody in Harlem started selling drugs again. 113th street to 116th street and 8th avenue was to the dope fiend what Park Avenue in Spanish Harlem was to the mother on Welfare. Drugs was sold in the open with a wreck-less abandonment quarters were sold by the thousands. At least 10 people were selling 1000 quarters a day within those 3 blocks area. The beauty of it all was that you had the girls selling right along with the guys. You had Dancing Debbie, Jackie Q, and Ignap just to name a few; and they did just as the guys. They would take a young guy who did not know what they was about to get into, to a hotel in New Jersey and about 10 of them would gang rape him. They would make him give oral sex all night rather he wanted to or not. The girls went further than the guys because they would do it to the young girls also. They did this girl from Manhattan Avenue name Gwen so bad; they defecated on her, and she was never the same after that. The guys was never the same after that either. The guys and girls on 116th street were Gregory, Cisco, Noel, Holes, Eddie, Audrey, Pop, Moody, Fat Levey and Black Steve; none of these guys were over 20 years old and almost all of them were pulling down at least one grand a day each as take home money.; the same with the girls. Then you had a lot of people from the Bronx who started hanging on 116th street between 8th and Manhattan Avenue. The Bronx guys introduced the 116th street guys to the murder game. The young drug dealers on 116th street were cool guys but they were soft also. My homeboy Junior Boy, Apple Jacks oldest brother was one of the few stick up kids from out of my block. Junior Boy was about 5 feet 9 inches and brown skin with thick wavy hair; he would always have something in his hand that made you think he knew karate, like moon chucks, stars, swords and Karate gear on. Anyway he would stick up the 116th street drug dealers whenever he felt like it. Most of the times when the 116th street dealers saw Junior Boy enter the block they would clear the street; until he left the block. The New Jersey stickup kids would also rob the dealers on 116th street. Then there were the Brooklyn stickup kids that would come victimize 116th street too. Every so often 116th dealers would catch one of the stickup kids out there and you would have about 100 people beating on one guy. The guy would look so pitiful out there all alone. 122nd street never had much trouble with stickup kids after our years of hunting them down and punishing them street justice style. However, I do remember one stickup kid got caught out there after sticking up Cockeyed Mike on our block. Well we chased that chump into the arms of the police and just when the guy thought he was safe we beat the hell out of him right there in the arms of the police. There was nothing the two cops could do. We were on 122nd street around building 222 that's near the corner of the block coming from 7th avenue and Mike was yelling at the cops that nigger tried to rob me while the cops had the guy in back of them Harry reached over and punched the guy in the eye Buddy slapped him while Little Larry was pushing the police out the way so that he could get at the guy. The police back up came and they were able to get the poor sap in the police car; which took him around the corner to the 28th precinct. Most times we would run around 123rd street to the precinct from 8th avenue to meet the police car from our block. Man I tell you, we were some real crazy people, and don't let some fool come messing with us for whatever reason we would not be satisfied until we got our man. I remember one night in late July of 1973 at around 8pm. I was in the P.A.L. on 123rd Street, at a party there the music was pumping and the girls were jumping, Smokey Robinson had "turn the light down low" blowing and I had those young girls trying to get real close to them. I was 21 at the time but all I wanted was a young girl about 16 to 20 years old. And this was surely a young girl's party I mean they were wall to wall and I was sizing up this bad 17 year old red bone girl name Cheryl. We had already slow danced off some of the Manhattan's slow jams and I was feeling hard as Chinese Arithmetic. Anyway I thought I would step outside to smoke a joint of Buddha bless because old man Leroy Otis did not play that smoking refer in his place. Leroy was the guy who had all the young up and coming Basketball players. He ran the Church of the Masters on 122nd and Morningside. When we were kids and had some of the best 10 to 14 year old ball players in our area. Homeboy Buddy played for Leroy. I remember one time we was about 10 years old and Buddy was supposed to play in Puerto Rico with Leroy's team but could not go because his oldest brother and sisters could not find his birth certificate, we all felt bad for Buddy that day. Leroy Otis was a funny guy he would talk to you with his hand in his pockets jiggling a lot of change and say to you "hey Big Buddy" as we got older we learned that Big Buddy meant something else if you know what I mean. Well anyway I stepped out of the PAL's dance to get some fresh air and smoke a joint. The P.A.L. was 1/8th of the block on the odd number side of the street about five car lengths from the ARC Drug Center and 10 car lengths from the 28th precinct. So as I stepped outside at about 8pm on a Friday night I looked down 7th avenue and all was calm. I then turned to look up 8th avenue and I saw what seemed like a whole block of people running on 123rd street. When they got close to where I was trying to get some fresh air and smoke a joint I realized it was 122nd street. I put the joint back in my pocket sucked in as much air as I could in seconds, then ran down the five steps of the P.A.L. building. This put me in the front of the mad rushing crowd. Here I am running in the front asking everyone what happened; I heard someone say something like "they got Steve" and before I knew anything the 28th precinct had those swinging doors and my face and chest burst the doors wide open because the crowd had pushed me up to the precinct. Before you knew it we were right in front of the sergeants desk and everyone was yelling "where is Steve, we want Steve" There was about 50 black men women and teenagers there at the front desk of the commanding sergeant of the 28th precinct demanding the immediate release of Steve. Here I am trying to get Little Larry, Bernard, Rockie, Tex, Bulldog, Charlie B., Cockeyed Mike, my sister Rossetta, Bulldog girlfriend Vickie, Pat, Wonder, Cynthia, and her sister Carol and a host of others to calm down. Unbeknown to me while I was at the PAL's dance at about 7:45pm, Fat Black and Ignorant (FBI) was staking out the Singelton Bar on the corner of 122nd street and 8th avenue; the Bar was our hangout spot. The FBI was looking for Red Duberson who had hung up parole and was living on the lam. Red had ran from the FBI about three times. One time he pushed one of them down causing the G-man to break a leg as he made his escape. This act of bravery shown during the cause of a confrontation with the law department gained Red much respect from the homeboys in the hood. So as Fat Black and Ignorant had the bar staked out, Steve was unaware of their presence in the hood. Steve saw a player that owned him about $500, trying to sneak past our block. The guy was coming from 125th street so as he passed the grocery store that Jimmy brought from the white people that owned it when I was a kid. The white folks that owned stores in the hood all sold them and moved out at the same time in about 1966 through 1968. I wonder what kind of conspiracy that was. So this guy passes Jimmy's store going downtown and Steve sees him crossing the street across from our block. It's said Steve calls him and says "hey man where the fuck is my money?" And the guy who was from up around 146th street somewhere said "man I don't have it now but I'll give it to you when I get my next package" and Steve said "fuck that nigger you fucked up my package of dope and could have gotten me killed." The Feds were watching the both of them arguing from their stakeout position across the street on 8th avenue and 122nd and 123rd street. Well needless to say Steve started kicking that guy's butt to the point that Fat Black and Ignorant had to blow their cover to save this guy because Steve knew Karate and was doing his best to look like the Five Fingers of Death, as he beat this guy. Also the block started to get in on the ass whipping too. One thing you could count on about 122nd street back then was they would whip a strange person's butt if he needed it. So the FBI pulls Steve off this guy but, the block thinks Steve has a right to stay on the guy's butt and so they start coming at the two white FBI guys. By now the Feds have him in their car and with about 50 mad colored folks on a hot summer night in the heart of Harlem demanding that they release him. Well Steve's mob of loyal homeboys and girls made it to the precinct before the Feds car because the action took place on 122nd street corner of 8th avenue so everyone ran up 8th avenue to 123rd street then they turned the corner on 123rd street where the dry cleaners is crossing the even number side of the street to the odd number side of the street where I stood taking a break. The mob moved with the force of a hurricane clearing everything within its path; which included sweeping me up in its fury. For the feds to get Steve to the precinct they would have to travel down our block to 7th avenue wait on the light then turn left on to 7th avenue to 123rd street corner, then turn left again going up 123rd street to the precinct which is about $4/5^{th}$ of the block on the same side of the street as the PAL. So everyone from the block is in the 28th precinct yelling for the release of Steve. By now I'm trying to get Bernard, Little Larry, Bulldog, Al, Steve's girl Carol, Vickie, my sister Rossetta and everyone else to shut up so that I could talk with the desk sergeant. The FBI arrived with him as they walk inside the precinct with him, someone yells out "there goes Steve" come on Steve, and the crowd grabs him and takes him from the FBI agents. The two G-men are standing there with a dumb look on their faces, they never seen a gang of mad black people like this before. So as they snatched Steve from the G-men the white desk sergeant face got candy apple red as he stood looking down on this crazy group of Black people wilding out; the sergeant yelled out "get these niggers out of here" and it seems like those white police came popping out of the walls and up from the floors and started throwing people out of the precinct. Well needless to say, once again my chest and face was pushing the precinct doors open with a violent thrust. As I landed outside on the side walk I saw from the left corner of my eye. Elcid pushing a cop away from Bernard who they were beating up and then a group of cops jumped on Elcid. There were police from all over the city and they were beating everything black that night. I walked across the street from the precinct and acted like I lived there when two policemen approached me with their night sticks out ready to kick butts. As they approached me with their night sticks ready, I said "I live here and I'm going home." They left me there at someone's door and went on to find another victim. I made it back to 122nd street without getting beat up by the cops, but Little Larry, Bernard and some of the woman in the crowd were not so lucky. However no one went to jail not even Steve who later took on the nick name Kojack. Everyone went to Harlem Hospital to support our wounded and we took over the hospital for about 5 hours and the police never came to the hospital. I guess they said "them 122nd street niggers are some crazy niggers." Well, after the Steve incident and the 28th precinct incident, from then on the police would not come through our block, so we were able to sell drugs out openly without anyone getting arrested. We would throw each other quarters and bundles of drugs from one side of the street to the other to each other.

Than we took over the Singleton Bar on 8th avenue of our block which was located between two apartment buildings 3 doorways from the corner of 122nd street. There was this little guy about 5 feet 5 inches weighing about 155 pounds name Jimmy. It was said that he had snitched on a guy back in the days. Jimmy was bald headed and about 35 years old. The bar front was all glass and the entrance door was of glass with the bar on your right hand side as you enter and Jimmy would be there serving customers while his lady Candy sat at the head of the bar where Jimmy could keep an eye on her; every now and then she would sneak off with Lorenzo.

The bar became our new hangout spot, but most of the time I'd rather hangout in the soul food restaurant on the corner of my block. The restaurant was owned by Shorty I never knew his real name. Shorty stood about 4 ½ feet in height and his upper body was built like Popeye's body when Popeye ate spinach. Shorty and I were cool and he only allowed the guys to hang out there because of me. I remember telling Shorty "don't worry about anyone coming in here to rob you because I have your back" and Shorty would frown his face up like he was mad at me and say "man, I don't need no help I'm a crowd by myself". I would laugh until tears came from my eyes when Shorty would say that because here was this 4 ½ foot tall 35 year old man built like Popeye after eating spinach swearing to death to protect his property. The restaurant had all glass window front with seating only at the counter and I would always be seated at the end of the counter away from the door, as I learned from watching cowboy movies always face the door to see everything that comes in and out of the restaurant. I remember one time when Shorty called me to the front of the restaurant to look at Little Dickey as he walked by the restaurant. Dicky was about 30 years old and he was the neighborhood cheat. He would victimize anyone by cheating in the dice game or not paying you if you played a number with him and it came out. Well, Shorty said to me and mind you when Shorty was angry he sounded like he wanted to cry when he spoke. So Shorty points to Dickey who was walking past the restaurant and said 'see that nigger I loaned him $20 bucks a week ago and he will not pay me back my money." I said to Shorty do you want me to take care of it and Shorty said "hell no" I will catch up with that mother fucker one day. Well just as Shorty prophesied about a week later in October 1973 around 7pm who came walking into the restaurant asking for change for a Ben Franklin ($50) but Dicky. Shorty looks down to where I sat and made eye contact with me. It seems that every time something was to go off in the restaurant Shorty always made eye contact with me first. Well Little Dickey asked Shorty for change of a fifty dollar bill and Shorty with his crying voice said "nigger you owe me twenty dollars for about a month and you refuse to give me back my money, and now you come in here asking for change of a fifty, why I should kick your ass about my money." Shorty is on the serving side of the counter and Dickey is on the customer side standing about 5 feet 5 inches in height. That's why we called him Little Dickey. So Dickey tells Shorty to" shut the fuck up and give me change for a fifty" by then Shorty seem to have taken a Superman leap over the counter and grabbed Dickey by the shirt collar mind you Shorty has a very strong upper body build like Popeye after he eats a can of spinach. So Shorty has a hold of Dickey's shirt and is slowly pulling him over the counter. The next thing I see is Dickey raining down a shower of jabs to Shorty's face and Shorty has tighten his face to absorbed the storm of punches as he is feeling around with his free hand for anything to use on Dickey, Shorty grabs hold of a knife and just as he brings it up to plant it in Dickey; Dickey yells out "okay here is your money" and quickly goes into his pocket throwing a lot of bills on the table just as Shorty brings the knife up to stab him. Shorty see's the money and pushes Dickey away from the counter while releasing him and Shorty grabs all the money on the counter. Shorty then begins to count the money with both of his hands and stated "I knew I would get your punk ass one day, you borrow my money and walk past me without paying me my money back." Well, by the time he finish saying what was on his mind to Dickey, as he counted the money Dickey took the same leap Shorty used to grab him by the shirt collar over the counter to snatch the money from Shorty's hands and exit the restaurant in the same motion leaving Shorty with a dollar bill in his hand and in a state of shock as to what just happened. Shorty appeared frozen in time for a few seconds and then very slowly he turned to make eye contact with me and when our eyes locked on one another I burst out in laughter over the whole scene and Shorty began to shout at everyone in the restaurant "Get out, get out and I don't mean one or two, I mean the whole dam crew." We would leave the restaurant when Shorty demands that we get out and go down to the bar. As the drug game continue to be the number one source of income in Harlem, I kept hearing about some organized group of drug dealers and how they were looking to recruit people. I was ready and willing to sign up like one does for the army. In those days you had to know someone who had enough juice to bring you in; you could not just walk up to someone that was in organized crime and ask to join. Someone that was a made guy had to introduce you into the group. I wanted in so bad because it was the times I had been waiting for a while in training as I loved to watch the gangster movies with Edward G. Robinson, Humphrey Bogart and James Cagney. Whenever I had a situation in the streets or when I got arrested I would always think about how they would handle the situation in the movies and I would go at it the same way; however I did not use a gun as freely as gangsters did in the movies, I only used a gun when someone was trying to use a gun on me. I had this experience when I had my first shoulder holster for my gun and Joseph McDuffie explained to me "Larry, whatever you do never get caught with the holster on" and with that in mind one day I went to a party at the Factory West club on 125 street between 8th and St. Nicholas avenue which is now a Bingo Hall. Well, I had my gun a 38 revolver and my holster on and I tried to get into the club but the security noticed it and would not let me in, so I headed back to 122nd street by way of St. Nicholas ave, which is the short cut to the block and it is a isolated area. When I got to 123rd street and St. Nicholas I saw this brother coming up the street and I intentionally bumped into him and when he said "yo man watch where your walking", I whipped out the 38 from its holster and the brother said to me "you're going to kill me because you bumped into me". That question made me stop and reflect for a moment and I looked at the brother and said no man I am not going to kill you. From that experience I promised myself that I would only carry a gun if I had trouble worthy of needing a gun.

In 1971 the drug game was the main source of income for Harlem. In February of 1972, I was arrested and sentenced to four months on Riker's Island for possession of a bundle of $2 dollar bags of heroin; the police found my heroin stash in a garbage can in the basement of building 240 in 122nd street. A bundle held 15 $2 dollar bags. While serving time I meet and became friends with Pop from 116th street. It was his first time on Riker's Island and my third. I had did two bids for breaking into stores when I was strung out on heroin during 1968 to 1970. Anyway there was this booty bandit from uptown name Marty and he was trying to make a move on Pop not because Pop looked feminine or act that way, it was because the creep knew that Pop was new at the jail game. Marty never made a move on Pop while I was with him; but when my three months out of four months was up I told Pop that the punk would be coming for him and he should just go off swinging and yelling curse words at him when he makes his move. Pop came home a few months after me and told me it went just as I said it would. Marty is lucky Pop and I did not come at him when we got out from Riker's, because we would have hunted that creep down and gave him the business.

CHAPTER 7

During the four months Riker's Island bid, I read some of the Bible for the first time and after reading the new Testament I walked away with the name "LOVE GOD", and when I was released if you wanted my attention you had to address me as Love God. This was around the time when the youth were spray painting on walls, trains, buses and everywhere. So I wrote my new name LOVE GOD throughout 122nd street on the building walls. In the summer of 1972 the movie Super-Fly burst on the scene with the soundtrack "Super-Fly and I'm your pusher Man" and we ran with it like young fools as we victimized each other through our selling of drugs. I sold drugs for the money but I never liked doing it because my three brothers Kaye, Greg and Pee Nut were hooked as well as my sisters Rosetta and Anne. There were so many of my family members and friends hooked on drugs and all our customers looked like me. From the movie Super-Fly there was another song on the sound track called "little child running wild". Curtis Mayfield made the soundtrack to the movie and it's said that he came up with the lyrics while reviewing the movie. Anyway the song said "little child running wild watch a while you see he never smiles". I felt that Curtis Mayfield was not only talking about the character in the movie who was hooked on drugs; but also the dealers in the movie, which made me think of myself and those I knew that were selling drugs to our brothers and sisters. To me we all were running wild hurting one another. Also what I learned from the movie Super-Fly was the difference in the two lead characters; which is what I witnessed around me, the character Super-Fly wanted out of the ghetto and he saw that selling drugs for a while would enable him to stack enough money to be able to pay his way out of the ghetto. He did not like what he was doing and felt the pain of his people. Then there was his partner in crime Fast Eddie who did not care who he hurt just as long as his needs were getting met. He was living the Ghetto Prince life and was willing to kill anyone who threaten his way of life. As a drug dealer I embraced the position of Super-Fly as the song says "ask him his dream what does it mean he don't know but he can't be like the rest was the most he would confess because the time is running out and there is no happiness." In Harlem we only took the negative aspects of the movie and soundtrack to Super-Fly. Everyone began sniffing cocaine off an album cover playing music while having sex and selling drugs to each other that much more.

In 1973, I was shot in the chest by Bernard for pulling a stupid joke on him while I was drunk. I did not deserve to be shot for pushing him down, but it served me right because lots of the seniors in 122nd St. would often come whisper to me "Larry leave these niggers alone because they don't like you" and I would respond "these are my friends". I had to learn the hard way that most of the people my age in 122nd St. could not stand me, but knew that they might need my violent ways, so they acted like they liked me in case they needed my violent behavior. I could not handle drinking in spite of trying every day. It would be years later when I learned that my father Moies Coldwell drunk every day and he could not handle alcohol no more than I could. While selling drugs on 122nd street I would not start drinking until 5pm and by 8pm I was sure to play stupid jokes on anyone that I came into contact with. I made lots of people dislike me during my drunken stupor period. Well I continued to hear about this organize crime gang and wanted so much to join. Mind you Nickey Bonds came to my mother's house almost every three months looking for his daughter who was a very close friend to my sister Anne. His daughter hung out on the block with us because she was going out with Black Brown.

I again set up shop at Shorty's restaurant and he was glad to have me back on the scene. One evening in November 1973 while holding down Shorty's restaurant this drug addict came in the restaurant for shelter because it was snow everywhere and cold. Shorty had told the person to leave his store and she would not take Shorty seriously. Every time he asked her to leave or he will hurt her she would say "ah go on Shorty" so about the fifth time Shorty asked her to leave and she said "ah go on Shorty"; Shorty threw a pot of hot coffee water on her and she ran out from the restaurant screaming and when I ran to the door to see where she went because the precinct is right on 123rd street which is the direction she was turning and there was a trail of smoke emanating from her body because of the hot coffee water and very cold weather. There was always something jumping off at Shorty's restaurant and I was the first one he would look at before or after it went down. A few months later Shorty's cook burned up the pork chops on the menu and when Shorty spoke to him about it he took Shorty's 4 ½ feet height for granted and responded to Shorty and said "shut the fuckup about the pork chops just buy some more." I don't know why people seem to overlook the fact that Shorty's waist line was built just like Popeye when he eats a can of spinach. Well Shorty reached in his pocket and came out with a 38 revolver in his right hand and with his left hand he reached up and grabbed the cook by his pant's belt and Shorty began to pistol whip the hell out of the cook. When the cook manage to free himself from Shorty Popeye like grip he ran straight to Sydenham Hospital for medical attention which was on 123rd street and Manhattan Avenue. Shorty looked at me as if he wanted my approval or if he was sending me a message. I always knew that Shorty could be just as violent as any of us out there when it concerned our money. Well about two hours later the cook enters the restaurant with a patch on the left side of his head and his right arm was in a sling like it was broken. The cook also had a cop on each side of him and the cops called out "who is Shorty." To my surprise Shorty stepped up over the counter and said "I'm Shorty" the police asked Shorty "did you pistol whip this guy" and Shorty said "you damn right I did it the nigger burnt my pork chops and started talking shit about it." I'm sitting there watching the scene play out and before I could advise Shorty the cops said "where is the gun" and Shorty responded "it's here in my pocket." And like a bolt of lightning the police was all over Shorty and before I knew it they had Shorty with each one of them holding those Popeye like arms of his and his feet were dangling in the air as they carried him out of the restaurant, he was charged with an assault with a dangerous weapon; the restaurant was closed while Shorty was in jail.

When I think back to life on 122nd street I questioned why I had become so violent. Unbeknown to my jive ass homeboys I never liked fighting and only begun fighting when they threw our clothes in the basement. I remember when I was eight years old and liked playing with the girls kissing and feeling on them. I did not like fighting in spite of the fact that I had a very good punch and could take a good punch. One day as a kid, old man Freddy who use to run the dice game next to Singleton's Bar on 122nd street and 8th avenue hired me to be the person to give the police from the 28th precinct a $10 dollar bill every hour so that they would not break up the dice game Freddy was running. He cut the game and would receive 10% of whatever was in the pot. When the dice shooter did not like the dice he was shooting with he would throw them across 8th avenue to St Nicholas side of the avenue and it was my assignment to track the dice down and retrieve them for Freddy because they were loaded dice meaning that once a shooter shot a good pair of dice and made a 4, 5, 6, 8, 9 or 10 then the loaded dice would be placed in the game by Freddy which only come up 7 would cause a shooter with anyone of 4, 5, 6, 8, 9, or 10 to 7 out losing the game. I worked for Freddy until I was about 12 years old. I began hanging with Mad Daddy in 1962. We became Five Percenters and did not eat pork or like the white man because he was unfair to Blacks. My brother Kaye also became a Five Percenter which means "A Poor Righteous Teacher." However I would eat my mother's pork chops at home but I did not eat pork skins or anything with pork in it outside of our home. The Five Percenters hangout was on 126th street and 7th avenue on the west side of the street, is where the founder Clearance Williams the third known as Puddin hung out before he was arrested and served time in Mattawhon Correctional Facility now known as Fishkill. We were kids and tried to get an adult to take me and Mad Daddy to visit Puddin, but were never able to. It was as a Five Percenter that I learned that I had the good gift of gab. I knew my lessons and could stand with anyone rapping off the 36 degree about WB Farrah coming to North America. There was one lesson I found just as relevant today as when I first heard it and that was "the TV is the one eye devil." It still only depicts black people as clowns, entertainers and criminals. The Five Percenters and the Muslim brothers use to go at it verbally. They did not like us because Puddin known as Allah to a Five Percenter was an off shoot of the Muslim Community. I remember when Malcom X was assassinated and his body was at Unity Funeral Home on 126th and 8th avenue. My boys and I went to view his body and an older Muslim brother told me if I wanted to see my mother I better get the hell out of there. I did not like the Muslim brothers because they did not like Puddin or Malcom X and also if you were not a Muslim you could not rap to a Muslim sister; but the Muslim brothers could rap to any and all of the sisters. I found most of the Muslims I knew as a Muslim at the time did not live out the life they professed to believe in.

Shorty made bail and two days later the restaurant was back open and Shorty was making eye contact with me on his every move. I said to him "Shorty man you never tell a cop you have a gun on you." Shorty said "your right." As I again reflect back to my life as a low lever drug dealer in Harlem, there were days when I made about $300 dollars a day and days when I only made $150 dollars for the day. It's an up and down game. I was sitting in the back of Shorty's restaurant one day when Black Bart came in telling me "yo, Love God, I just got finished talking with that nigger Nicky Bonds." I said "what you talking about man?" Black Bart was dating Nicky's daughter for the past three years and he would often take her money and jewelry from her. On this day Black Bart whose real name was Lawrence Brown, tells me "yeah man that nigger come telling me to leave his daughter alone because she is getting married in a few weeks." Mind you in my community I was known as being crazy but I was never stupid. I asked Black Bart "and what did you say?" He said "I sucked my teeth and rounded on that chump." Mind you 122nd street was not afraid of any name throughout Harlem but I understood clearly what money could do and Nicky had money in great big old stacks. So I said to Bart "you should have showed Nicky more respect than what you did because he has enough money to have this restaurant wiped off the map and further more I am going to the movies." Whenever the block got hot my boys, Tony, Bulldog, in the days Ray Day, Apple Jack and others would go hangout in the West End movies theater on 125th street between Morningside and Manhattan Avenue. We got in free because one day we walked in without paying to see a karate movie and the manager called the police on us; the movie was cut off and we were escorted out of the theater by about 20 policemen, and I had everyone wait around 125th street and Manhattan Avenue by the train station until the last police car had left the theater and then we marched right back in the West End catching the manager off guard. As he saw about nine of us come right back in the theater he was at a loss for words and could not believe our crazy boldness. I said to him as we marched in "just like we are back now call the police again and we will be back just like we are here now and the next time I am going to take that diamond stick pin" that he had on his tie. So from that day on when we needed a break from the block we would hideout in the West End movie theater. So we were not in the theatre more than 15 minutes when Tex, and Buddy came running in there calling out my name "Love God, Love God guest what happened?" "What happened?" I said as cool and calm as I could. Tex began explaining that Nicky came to the restaurant with this big brother who stood at 6 feet 3 inches and weighed 275 pounds and moved like a ballerina. He has a big reputation for doing serious work throughout Harlem. Tex said Brown was walking out the restaurant door just as Nicky and his hit man were coming into the joint and Nicky said to the hit man, "there goes Brown get him" as he pointed Black Bart out to the hit man. The hit man jumped on Brown with a 357 magnum in his right hand and a pair of brass knuckles on his left hand. He beat Brown with the magnum and brass knuckles for about 5 minutes I am told, beating his head into the wall then he stopped hitting Brown who was trying to absorb the death blows from a 275 pounds professional hit man on Browns 5 feet 10 inches and 150 pounds. He stopped hitting Brown and cocked the magnum and that's when Tex, and Buddy ran the hell out of the restaurant on their way to me. They did not leave when my guys and I did because Tex said "that nigger Nicky ain't fucking with 122nd street.' It's said that after the hit man put the beat down on Black Bart with the brass knuckles and the 357 he cocked the hammer on the 357 to shoot Black Bart in the head and Nicky said "no don't kill him just whip his ass." During all this, Shorty was in the back of the restaurant frying a can of beans and never came out of the kitchen. About a week later Black Bart was sitting in the restaurant with his head wrapped jaw broke and left arm broke, and he would tell everyone that asked 'I deserved what happened." I told him "any nigger beat me like that must kill me because I'm coming back at him with nothing but a water gun and lye in it if I have too." Black Bart was never the same after that beat down and he began to display psychotic behavior and delusional thinking. One day we were at his house on 120th street and 8th avenue over the Boulevard Bar where we sometimes hung out and out of nowhere Black Bart jumped out of his second floor window to go to the store. He landed all right but his mental capacity was affected by the ass whipping he received. He was gunned down in 1975 for robbing a dice game on the block so I was told.

In the summer of 1974 my Zaytuna came from college for the summer break and the two of us would try to spend as much time together as we could. So I did not have time for my young girl who lived on 121st street between 7th and 8th avenuc. I liked her a lot but Zay was my college love. She spent the whole summer begging me to go back to Winston Salem with her. She promised to get me into college and show me a new life other than Harlem's drug selling, using and daily violence. The two of us was sitting on a bench in Morningside Park that looked straight into 122nd street, my block. I had this delusion that 122nd street was my block and that the people in it had love for me. It did not matter that the mothers and fathers of the block would often pull me to the side and tell me "Larry, leave those niggers alone, they don't like you and they don't mean you no good." I would always respond to them "all ma those are my friends," and the mothers and fathers would walk away shaking their heads as if they were saying (it's a damn shame this nice poor fool has to learn the hard way). I would always protect the elders and children on my block and I would punish anyone in my age group that got out of line with the elders or messed with the children. Well in about April 1974

Mr. Buddy was the blocks handyman and he was the strongest man on the block. He would ask you for a handshake and squeeze the hell out of your hand until you say "uncle;" letting you know he was the strongest on the block. So one day the two of us had it out now mind you I was 22 years old and looked like16 years old and Mr. Buddy was about 35 years old. So here the two of us are in the middle of the street face to face with Mr. Buddy trying to force me to shake his hand so that he could make me submit by saying "uncle." At this point of my 122nd street career it was understood that you did not fuck with that crazy nigger Love God unless you were ready to kill him, because I was real good with my fight game. So here we stand face to face with Mr. Buddy wanting a handshake. He said "Larry shake my hand" and I said "man get out of here with that bullshit." This went on until he grabbed me by my shirt and I did what I learned watching karate movies in the West End theatre to him. I grabbed him in the chest with both hands and fell backwards placing both of my feet in his midsection and just like in the karate movie I flipped his ass in the air and over me, and when he landed on his butt he had enough and got the hell out of my face. It was a friendly standoff and the flip was all it took to send the message that he was no longer the strongest nigger on the block. Zaytuna and I sat about three avenues away from my beloved 122nd street. With her trying to convince me to give it up and I said "girl I am not leaving my block they love me there." She responded for the first time like the mothers and fathers of 122nd street that tried to get me to see that the only people on 122nd street who had love for me was those that were trying to get me to wake the hell up and get the hell out of there before I got killed or killed someone. Little did I know that after the summer of 1974 I would not see Zaytuna for twenty three years. I liked her because she was the only girl I knew at the time that was in college. Once she returned to school my 121st girl and I picked up where we left off at. Other than my childhood girlfriend Pipes, I really did not like dating the females on 122nd street. I like to think that I could have had my pick of females on 122nd street, because I was a good dresser. We learned how to dress at 10 and 11 years old. We would go downtown and steal clothing material like pepper silk, mohair and raw silk and take it to Mr. Tony's Tailor shop on 125th street between 7th and Lenox Avenue to have our pants Tailor made and get our shirts from A. J. Lester's men's store on 125th between 8th and 7th avenue down from the Apollo and Lowe's movie theatre near 8th avenue. Also I had a good rap and look good as well. We had lots of beautiful woman on 122nd street but to tell the truth I was a bit immature for my age in terms of wanting to settle down with a woman and have babies. So other than Pipes, Zaytuna and that time with Hanteria, I really did not have a girlfriend from my block. I must say to that perhaps the women on my block stayed away from my crazy but after witnessing many of my crazy antics on 122nd street. In August of 1974, I recall leaving my sister Carolyn's house on 121 St. on 7th avenue heading to 8th avenue and about to go in the block when for the first time in my life I had this experience where I heard a very quiet and still voice say to me "Larry one day you will have to give an account for your behavior." I heard it clearly and accepted it as it was said, but I paid it no mind once I turned the corner heading to 122nd street on 8th avenue. Well, in October of 1974 Bulldog, Scrubb and I were arrested for murder. As I look back to the extreme level of violence I often found myself involved in for the most part no reason of my own but for protecting a block that was never really mine and some negroes who might not have even come to my funeral had I gotten murdered out there, I wish to the God of my understanding today that I could have seen and understanding the warnings that the seniors gave me, and took heed to their warnings. So here the three of us were in the 28th precinct for the death of a stick up kid. Mind you that a stick up kid's life was always facing death for robbing a drug dealer. It was the law of the street that if you stick someone up they could punish you at whatever level of violence they deem necessary and whenever they were able to get the upper hand on the stick up kid. Being a stick up kid in Harlem in the 70's gave you a very short life span. This stick up kid had not victimized us but he was threatening.

As we sat in the precinct I saw that it would be best for me if I got rid of Bulldog and Scrubb. Bulldog and I were partners in a drug deal at the time of this case and he was in possession of the work (drugs). I said to them don't say a word I will do all the talking. Bulldog and Scrubb were released and I was sent to Riker's Island for 18 months to deal with the legal aspects of the Manslaughter case and I never heard from Bulldog and Scrubb after that.

CHAPTER 8

I eventually received 6 to 18 years for the body and I really did not mind because I regret to this day what happened to the stick up kid there in that hallway, because chances are, he would have never came at me at anytime to rob me or people around me. Those 18 months on Riker's Island was a learning period for me. While waiting for court on Riker's Island I learned to fight with control and my thinking at that time was "fuck the world". I was the only one on Riker's Island from my neighborhood and I had to represent. I remember running out of money and did not have cigarettes so I stopped smoking until I got money for cigarettes, rather than asking people for a cigarette every time I wanted to smoke without having cigarettes. You see begging while your incarcerated from training school to jails, is a sign of weakness and it will lead to someone or ones trying to victimize the bagger. So that crazy Love God knew not to place himself in a situation like that. I learned when I was 13 years old and sucked my thumb for 13 years, and one day while in Bellevue for the second time, I woke up the next morning and was sucking my thumb and this guy saw me and said "Larry if they (the older guys) see you sucking your thumb they are going to fuck you." Well I took my thumb out of my mouth and never sucked my thumb again in life. From that experience I learned that whatever habit I found myself hooked on I could overcome it once I made my mind up.

So instead of begging for a cigarette every time I wanted to smoke I just stopped smoking until things got better. During my Riker's Island experience Harold Melvin and the Blue Notes came out with a song called "Where are all my friends." This song really hit me hard because I felt like they were singing about my experience with every example they gave in the song. The only people who stood by me during this experience were my 121st street young girl Cynt and Steve. It was at this point that I begin to reflect back to the mothers and fathers on 122nd street that told me "those niggers are not your friends." As for my mother she was burned out from all of the juvenile facilities she supported me and my brothers Kaye, Greg and Pee Nut with visits also my siblings were fighting their own addictions and sense of hopelessness. So here I was with a body charge and just Cynt and Steve was my support. I became very angry at the world and took on the molto of "fuck the world." I was one of the forty inmates that started contact visits on Riker's Island in December of 1974 because the Tombs won the law suit to have contact visits and they had shut down the Tombs in about November 1974. So whoever was in the Tombs at the time of the law suit qualified for contact visits if they were on Riker's Island; and I was in the Tombs in October and sent to Riker's island in November of 1974. My young girl Cyn**t** came to visit often while she was just 17 years old. I remember while on a visit with her I wanted to ask her to sneak some reefer in for me by putting it into balloons and in her mouth so that when we kissed she could pass it to me. But the one time I tried to speak those words and looked into her innocent beautiful face, I could not bring those ignorant words out of my mouth. I saw her not knowing anything about breaking the law and getting into a world of trouble for stupid me and I did not want that on my conscious, so for the rest of that visit I never said anything to her regarding braking the law. She was supportive of me for 7 ½ years of my incarceration and that ignorant thought never came back to my mind. I remember when we first started dating and I offered her some reefer and a drink of champagne and she said that she did not do those things and I never ever offered her any of that again for our 27 years of relationship. My brother, Kaye came to see me one time and brought me some reefer by having it sewn into the cuffs of the pants he left for me to wear to court. I did not know that our visit together in the spring of 1975 would be the last time we would see each other face to face in this life ever again. Kaye was a year younger than I was and we had grown up in the streets hand in hand. In fact Kaye was the only guy I have ever been jealous of. He learned to tell time before me and everyone that met him always liked him. He used to run con on white folks that he meet downtown and bring them home with him. They would give all of us money at seven and nine years old. I recall one time I was about ten or eleven years old and Kaye took our mother to the Apollo to see James Brown and to dinner at the steakhouse next door to the Apollo. When my sister Doris told me where they were after I asked her for mommy, I felt like she told me Kaye had taken Pipes out to the Apollo and dinner. I found out what time they should be coming home and I hid in a building in the dark shadow doorway on 123rd street and 8th avenue waiting for them to come from 125th street and about 9PM they came near the building I was waiting at and I jumped out of the dark shadow and spat in Kaye's face out of jealousy. He was always a year or two ahead of me and he was a much better hustler than I was; and in my mind I was one of the best. I stopped hanging out with Kaye at about twelve years old because I became embarrassed to have my mother come pick the both of us up from the precinct when we were arrested. I loved my brother Kaye and wished that he could get himself off that heroin. One thing about Kaye was that when he got hooked onto drugs he was not able to break away from it like I was. Kaye was my man and I remember one time in 1972 when I could not find my drugs in the house I thought Kaye stole them. I hit him and he picked up a bottle of bleach and went off on me. I got some bleach in my eyes and ran over to Sydenham Hospital. Kaye was my brother and my man; I found my stash later when I got back from the hospital but I was glad Kaye won that fight we had.

Well here I am now going to court once a month for the body in October of 1974 and after the judge remanded me I exited the courtroom and turned to the judge and said "you kiss my ass". I was feeling the fuck the world statement real strongly and felt that I had no hope and nothing else to lose. I got into an argument with another inmate that was in five Block when we were in the receiving room one day after returning to Riker's Island from Court. We had a argument about what I don't recall. He was sent to his Block and I was sent to mine three Block. So one day I was going to the gym which is down the prison hall by the commissary pass all the blocks, so when we got to five block I saw the guy I had some words with. I called him to the cell block gate and asked him "why was he talking so much shit to me a few days ago" He began to talk lots of jive to me while he was behind the cell block door bars and before he knew what hit him I had punched him in the face straight through the cell bars, he was shocked and kept saying "that nigger punched me through the bars, that nigger punched me through the bars." My reputation as a crazy kick ass nigger on Riker's Island, began to spread through all 8 cell blocks and everybody knew not to mess with me. I reunited with a childhood friend named Bit whose girl friend kept us supplied with reefer by sewing it in the cuffs of Bit's pants that he got on a visit. Bit and I ran together when we were eleven to fourteen years old. We used to go around 59th street to 23rd street robbing cash registers and stole anything worth value that was not tied down. Here we were together again in three block. Bit walked with a limp after being shot by the police at seventeen years old for robbing Token booths in Harlem. He used to live on 121st between 7th and 8th Avenue and moved to 142nd street between 7th and Lenox Avenue where he learned to rob Token booths. Most of the stick up kids lived past 135th street or on the Eastside of Harlem and everyone else sold drugs. What seem to always trouble me is the fact that so many of us made the same stupid and dumb choices of selling drugs, robbing and a few took to kidnapping drug dealers. It was well known and understood that the kidnap game guaranteed you a very short life because the punishment for kidnapping on the streets was death by any means necessary. So Bit and I had lots of reefer thanks to his girl friend. One day in April of 1975 while working on the paint gang I was painting in 7 block, and when I climbed up onto the scaffold reaching the second tier I looked in a cell and there was this guy sitting on his bed with his feet swinging off the floor and his head down and both hands clasped together seeming as if he was in a heavy state of worrying and as I looked at him closer, I recognized PeeWee. PeeWee came from 114th street in the block where Watley High School is between 7th and 8th Avenue. They sold quarter bags of heroin for $75 dollars a bag and some people from that area on 116th street to 113th street sold one thousand quarters a day. They were getting real money for drugs in that neighborhood. PeeWee was always known to walk through the neighborhood with his basketball hoping to become an NBA player. However, PeeWee did not grow after he hit 5 feet, 5inches, in height and with his hopes of becoming an NBA player dreams being shattered he worked a few community center jobs and was one of the few guys in our age group who graduated from high school. I remember one day back in 1972, I went to buy some quarters from 115th street to break them down into duce bags of heroin which is what we sold on my block. A full quarter spoon of good heroin mixed at $75 dollars brought me seven bundles of fifteen two dollar bags in a bundle giving me $210 dollars from spending $75 dollars for the quarter and I would always buy about ten quarters at a time. So I hear that this drug label ARC is the best thing going on 115th street. And when I get there I see about

LARRY LUV

35 guys trying to cop from some dude in the middle of them and as I get a good look at the dealer it was PeeWee. So here he is in a cell on Riker's Island for the first time in his life ever being in jail or arrested for any criminal behavior. I like to think that God was working on his and my behalf because we needed each other. PeeWee would hang out with some of the guys from my block but stayed away from me, and I had no one from my block there other than Bit who left the neighborhood as a kid. So here were the both of us PeeWee and I, and he had a body as well. There was a gang war to take over 115th street by some guys from Brooklyn and PeeWee got caught out there protecting his Block. PeeWee and I spent most of the 7 ½ year prison time together on Riker's Island, Comstock, Nap and was roommates in Fishkill for about 2 years together. He is one of the smartest guys I know. As we stood there glad to see one another and without saying a word, PeeWee and I bonded for life.

So here I am on Riker's Island for six months in April of 1975 and building a reputation as a kick ass nigger. There was lots of action going down at Riker's. If you had cash some guards would bring you whatever you wanted within reason; like drugs, knives to use on each other. You have to have access to a knife if the fight went bad. I made knives while working in the paint gang. I would get a metal fork or spoon and cut the head off them, then grind it down to a sharp point and give them to the homeboys when they came on the Island. I stayed in possession of a knife throughout my 7 1/2 years in prison but I never had any intention to stab or cut anyone, because my knuckle game was good enough for me and everyone I had beef with. I kept the knife in case someone pulled one out on me or tried to jump me; but I would much rather use my fist to settle those foolish issues that now and then presented themselves plus once I got smoked up all I wanted to do is laugh. The funniest times were when the inmate would play the 730 game which is the mental illness count; he would act like he was crazy to beat his court case and go to court and start crawling in the court room and barking like a dog or cat. Those were some very funny moments that I would laugh like crazy at them. There was this time when the CO would pack you up and send you to Sing Sing correctional Prison while you was still fighting your case, and I did not want to go to Sing Sing because my young girl could not visit me there. So this day the CO ordered me to pack my property and get on the bus for Sing Sing. Now mind you, the inmates did not have a choice rather they wanted to go or not. There were times when some inmates would refuse to go and the COs would gas them up and beat their butt all the way to Sing Sing. So here I am the F the world bad nigger on Riker's being told that he must go to Sing Sing rather he wants to or not, so I striped butt naked and came out of the cell I was being housed in carrying my property. I was ordered by the COs to put my clothes on but I refused to get dress and they walked me throughout Riker's Island and placed me in the Box for about two weeks, and after the two weeks I was sent back to 3 block and not to Sing Sing. I eventually got transferred to six block and began to meet guys that had connections to the Black Mafia; it was Frank Johnson known as Randy, Skiter Boy and Mikey. We would talk about organizing when we got out and what our roles would be in the organization. Here is another funny moment, one day while we were sitting on the ledge of the first floor cell door on the B side of six block talking about organized crime, this Spanish guy walks past us with a pair of zebra stripped punk panties on and no shirt walking a rat on a rope man we almost passed out laughing at the scene. Yes six block is where I finally met the organized crime Black Mafia. I learned from them about the Godfather of Boston road and how everyone bows to him. I met him after coming home, and he was a cool guy and a fair brother to me. Anyway we all were talking about what each of us will offer the organization; and I thought to myself that I would be the hit man for the organization, but the more I thought about it the more I realized that a hit man is expendable and I wanted to be of value to the organization and also I am not, nor ever have been a killer, and so that foolish thought never came back to my head. I was just a soldier of the streets fighting in the battle of the Shateu Briond in hopes of surviving the life of poverty as a black male in an unfair social system. I received my share of pain like when I was shot in the chest by Bernard who was one of those people that the older folks in my block tried to warn me about, and I still carry the bullet under my left arm to this date, and in 1971 the director of PS 144 after school who stood at about 6 3" and 190 lbs sucker punched me and fractured my jaw, but he lost the fight because I went buck while on his ass. There was also that moment in 1969, when Imp the Dimp's father cut me on the arm with a 007 knife in a dice game when he was cheating and I took my leather coat off to fight him in hopes of keeping him from cutting my coat. I must say that he did not really want to cut me because he only hit me on the arm with the knife and not slice my arm.

Imp the Dimp's father was a dope fiend when we were kids and he eventually turned his life around in about 1980 and begin talking about this guy name Jesus Christ and how he can change people's lives from what I heard while serving time. However, at some point while on Riker's Island, I learned to make my point while fighting without fighting like a mad man and I also learned to stop and think before I act and I was no longer a re-actionist as well as I learned who my true friends are. Well Skiter, Randy, Mikey and I would spend lots of our time talking about white gangsters and the few black gangsters. I learned about Reggie Ceborn and Hollywood Harold and how jokers would pay punk dues to them to keep the pressure off of them. What I learned from them is that most of the tough guys moved from Harlem to the Bronx in the early sixties. It was Frank Johnson who came from New Jersey and had the heart of a gunfighter and the life experience, and Skiter Boy whose brother brought his mother a home when he was a teenager which motivated us to dream as teenagers to do the same in Harlem, and Mikey B was the smoothest guy I had ever ran into at the time. He could recognize a C.O. who would be open to being corrupted in a heartbeat. One day in 1975 Randy, Skeiter and I, decided to go to the Chapel for church service to see what new persons had been put on Riker's Island. The Chapel is where most of all the new inmates would come to meet up with their homeboys. So here we are and I see these two Prison Ministry guys talking about this Jesus Christ guy. I noticed that these are the same guys that I first met in Warwick State training school and the Annex training school, and now here they are talking about this Jesus guy. The next thing I knew was that I had came forward to accept Jesus Christ as my Lord and Savior. I had no idea just want that meant and why I did it. Well in about October of 1975 my man Bit was sentenced to 5 to 10 years and sent up state. Pee Wee was in 7 block going to court once a month. I would stop by his block to talk with him by giving the CO some paint when he asked for it and also the CO liked me as a kick ass brother and would allow me to visit Pee Wee in the cell block from time to time. So we kept supplies of drugs there on Riker's. As my name continue to spread from Riker's to most of the prisons that were waiting on me to come upstate. In 1976 we had the first riot since the Attica prison riot. All of the gangsters stayed clear of the riot and advised me to do the same which I did. However four days after being locked down for twenty four hours a day, I was let out of my cell for a few minutes to walk around and when it came time to go back into my cell, I did not want to go back when instructed. The C.O. asked me to go back to my cell and I was not willing to go. This C.O. and I did not like each other and for the most time I stayed clear of this creep; however, after being locked down for 96 hours and I finally got out of the cell for a few minutes, I was really not ready to go back in. So here is this foolish me and this creep C.O., standing face to face in a standoff position, mind you no one else is around because the prison has been locked down for the past 4 days due to the riot and all the other inmates in 6 block are locked in their cells. So here we stand this loud mouth foolish inmate and this big tall male correction officer, in a standoff. After a few seconds of face to face standoff, I thought about it and decided to go to my cell; however, my face changed its expression of fuck the world to okay I am going in my cell. The C.O. read the face expression as a sign that I was just a loud mouth punk like he thought all along and he grabbed me in the chest with both hands and when it was over his left eye was bleeding and he had punch marks in his face. I began to yell he hit his face on the cell bars. I was escorted to the holding Pen and thank God the media was there and they took pictures of the C.O. and pictures of me. So on that night of the C.O. assault they cornered me off into the receiving room by myself. Oh, yeah my tag still remained "fuck the world" in spite of accepting Jesus Christ as my Lord and Savior. I also continued to smoke reefer every chance I got. So here I sit in the receiving room by myself with no witnesses waiting to get my ass kicked. I was given a pencil and paper to write what happen. At about 2am the cell door opened and these four C.O.'s came marching into the cell in the receiving room where I was alone and waiting for them to arrive. They had on, kick a inmate's ass gloves as they entered the cell. I said to myself well Larry here it comes and I turned the pencil in a stabbing position because I was not going to allow any man to beat me up without putting up a strong fight. I slowly raised my head and looked into the eyes of the lead C.O. and we knew each other throughout my stay on Riker's, it was the 7 block CO that allowed me to visit Pee Wee. As our eyes met he stopped in his tracks and the others stopped in back of him. He then looked me in the eyes and shook his head from left to right about twice and turned around and walked out of the cell with the other three following him without a word spoken. I like to think that when he recognized me he did not want to hurt me or kill me. The both of us had a very good relationship and he was known to lead the hit squad there at Riker's. I'll share another theory about why they did not kill me that night later. After the hit squad left me without whipping my ass or killing me, later that night I was handcuffed and given a strong shot of Thorazine then handcuffed to the cell bars with my hands held high above my head leaving me to stand on my tip toes with my face up against the cell bars and once the Thorazine took effect my head and face danced on and off of the cell bars for the rest of the night.

I was placed in keep lock for about a month and eventually charged with an assault and received four years running with the body sentence of 6 to 18 years, which means that I would have to serve 6 years in prison before I qualify for parole consideration. They tried to get the sentence of 4 years running wild, but the Black judge kept saying "this boy already has 6 to 18 years, and he said it about 3 times before he made the 4 years run concurrent with the 6 to 18 years. A few weeks before the assault on the CO, my crew and I were in the chapel to see the new inmates. That was how you learned who had come to the Island. Well these guys, there was from this Christian volunteer group called PAL (Pals for Christ). There was this big white guy who said he was once a professional fighter name Chuck about 40 years old and this short black guy from Brooklyn named Russell and he claimed to be an X gang member from the 50's. What intrigued me about Chuck and Russell is that when I was in Warwick State Training School in 1966 they would come in telling us about this guy named Jesus Christ, and when I was in the Annex State Training School in 1967-1968, Chuck and Russell would come bragging about this Jesus Christ guy there as well. I was only there in the church to see who was new in the facility and in the Annex the Pals for Christ used to bring these three fine young girls in my age bracket with them, so I would go to church there in the Annex to see those three fine sisters. Now remember my brother Kaye and I were some of the troublesome kids on 122nd street but we were brought up at the Saint Andrew Baptist Church on 132nd street between 7th and Lenox Avenue where our mother made us go with her when we were kids as often as she could take us. So here I come with my gangster crew to just see who is new on the Island and Chuck and Russell are here talking about turning your life over to God in the name of a brother called Jesus Christ. I like to think that Eddie Kendrick from the Temptations song " He was a friend of mine;" had something to do with my coming forward as well as the many times my mother made Kaye and us go to church with her. Mind you, in spite of my accepting Jesus Christ as my Lord and Savior their on Rikers Island, I continued my goal of becoming an American Black Gangster, by dreaming of living the Black Gangster life. We became a crew there in 1975 on Riker's Island and in September of 1976 Skiter, Randy and Mickey were sentenced and sent up state. Then Pee Wee stopped by my cell block one day and called out to me from behind the block cell bars, he told me he copped out to 6 to 18 years. We found ourselves laughing at the pain in his voice that day he yelled out to me "Yo, Love, 6 to 18 years"!

    I was contemplating going to trial until one night in my cell I saw the hand writing on the wall. You see three guys were in that first cell in 6, block on the B side of the block prior to me being in that cell and all three of them had bodies and they went to trial and blew trial ending up with twenty-five years to life. Now here I am in the same cell with the same charge and court appointed attorney thinking I am going to beat the case at trial when I knew in my heart that I was guilty. Also my trial judge was the one I had cursed out every time he remanded me and now I sat thinking about going to trial not to mention those two jokers that I cut loose in the precinct who might be potential witnesses against me at trial. So I manned up and accepted the 6 to 18 years they were offering.

CHAPTER 9

I was sent to Dannemora Clinton Prison in November of 1976 and for three months I smoked no reefer even when offered because Dannemora was well known to kill inmates. I remember reading Lucky Luciano Biography and he was in Dannemora and did not play with those mean crackers, so I played it very cool for those three months. I was trying to come to terms with 6 to 18 years during the 1976 world-series when Reggie Jackson hit those home runs at Yankee Stadium during the World Series. One night we were talking about when we go to the Parole Board through the bars to each other and everyone was talking about going to the Parole Board in about 6 months to 18 months from the date of our conversation and when they asked me "Love when, do you go to the Board," I said "in four years". I asked one guy who had did a bid before "how do you do 6 to 18 years", and he said "Love you count it by the seasons not the days." After two months I was sent to Comstock and a C.O. asked me if I was a celebrity because everyone was greeting me and seemed to be glad to see me there like misery loves company. One guy from Riker's said "Larry I am glad to see you now you can help me fight these niggers who keep coming at my girl (another inmate)." I heard him and thought he was crazy. My focus was how to do 6 to 18 years with a fine young soft sweetie waiting for me to come home. While in Comstock I began to learn a little more about Jesus Christ, but at nights when

I went to bed I would think about the fast money, cars and big leg girls. While at Danormora Clinton correctional facility, during orientation, I dropped the F the world mind set and begin longing for the day I would get my freedom back. I was never offered any reefer during my six months in Comstock either. I did not run into Skiter Boy, Randy or Mikey until about two years later. Pee Wee and I were in Comstock to Nap and again the drugs were flowing freely. I got Baptized at Nap in 1977. However, at night I dreamed of a gangster life as I read Lucky Luciano, Frank Costello, Vito Genovese and Carlos Gambino documentaries. As I look back today at my accepting Jesus Christ there in Riker's Island, yes, I had accepted Jesus Christ that day, but I had not surrendered my life to God in the name of Jesus Christ. So, I kept dreaming of that gangster life and smoking reefer whenever I could and I went to church on Sundays and prayed every night before I went to bed. While serving time I only had visits from my young girl and a friend from 122nd St. named Steve. The time was hard on my girl because she was 17 years old when I was arrested. One day in 1977 while in Nap, she wrote me a Dear John letter. I cried like a baby and wrote her back begging her to don't give me up. I also prayed to God to keep her in my life, but I knew it would be unfair to place my burden on her. In her dear John letter she said "I hope I taught you some things that will make you a better man for some woman one day".

    I became engrossed in learning about the gangster life during the day and prayed at nights before bedding down thinking about the gangster life. While at Nap a kid from my building name Richard Moore whom we called Trick who lived in 244 on the top floor came as well as Apple Jack who was a stick up kid from my block and his brother Junior Boy. Junior Boy and Apple Jack were arrested for robbing a jewelry store and the kid Richard Moore was in for drug dealing. We called Richard Moore, Trick because he had a basketball game that everyone thought was NBA ready.

WHO RAISED HIM

One day while in Nap, I was in my cell thinking about my past and how much of a man I thought I was out there in the streets of Harlem at 22 years old. My idea of being a man at that time was being able to sleep with any and every women who would say yes, and being able to out drink and fight any male who comes along. Well, as I sat there on the edge of the bed in 1978, in a one man cell there in South Hall, where I was being housed in and thinking about being a man and what the qualifications of manhood are. I began to cry quietly as I realized that I was so far away from being a man until it was a shame. You see, I had no positive male examples to learn from and no one ever spoke to me about what being a man entailed. All the older males in my community slept with as many women they could and drank just as much as I did. From that point in my life on at 26 years old, I began to rethink what being a man required a male to conduct himself as. My brother Greg started visiting me when he had gotten out of prison while I was in Nap. He smoked dust and he was high and got busted in the visiting room one Saturday while coming in to visit me. Greg was on parole and because of the arrest in Nap's visiting room he was sent to Green Heaven a few months later. I was also sent to Green Haven a week after Greg was arrested because I threw a jar at the lady C.O. who busted Greg in the visiting room that Saturday. The jar did not hit her and it was not because I did not try to hit her with it. I was glad to be in Green Haven because that is where they sent my brother Greg about 3 months after I was sent there. Green Haven was a very tough prison and I needed to look out for Greg. We both were on the West side of B block, and one day my brother Greg smacked this chump over a basketball game while playing in the yard. I admonished Greg and warned him to never smack a joker here in the face, you must knock fire out of him so that others would know that you are not the one. There was also an incident with Greg one day when we had to clean up all cells in the cell block and I noticed about five Spanish inmates talking in a conspiracy like huddle, which meant that they were getting ready to step to someone. As I observed the direction of their focus, and notice it was focus on my brother Greg. We both were housed in B Block and Greg cell was on the third floor and I was housed on the first floor; so I ran and got my knife from my stash and pulled Greg next to me with our backs to the wall as we waited for them to make the first move. Greg had the mop ringer and I had my knife and just as they began to approach us an older Spanish brother stepped in front of them and pulled them away from Greg and I. I learned that the beef was over Greg using the mop ringer and bucket too long and not allowing anyone else to use it. I admonished Greg and helped him to see that he was wrong. He went home after six months and I was never so glad because Green Haven was a very dangerous prison and they still had the death chair there as well as it was the most corrupt prison of them all. If you had money you could get whatever you wanted. Well as faith would have it I ran into Herm from the Annex State training school. He was on the prison boxing team in the Heave and very well known throughout the prison as a very good fighter. He was also serving time for a body and Skiter Boy introduced us to each other. Herm told Skiter Boy how him and I use to fight while in the Annex State Training School and that he won all the fights and I corrected him that he did not win all the fights we had. He did not argue the issue. The both of us did not have any beef there in the Heave and we hardly saw each other because he was on the East side of the Heave and I was on the West side. The both of us also knew that we were at the age where when two men come together in a fight it would most likely be a fight to the death and we had no beef and had out grown our youthful thinking to allow us to fight to the death for no real reason. Well, Frank Johnson, Skiter, and I continued to make plans for our crew when we got out. Frank Johnson went home in November of 1978 and got caught up in the dust game. He was arrested and they claimed he died trying to escape from Riker's Island in 1979. Skiter left for home in April of 1979 and he never sent a word back to me after promising that he would. I continue to study the lifestyle of gangster life and also my man Nut and Yaba and I banded together and went to school while in Green Haven and we received our GED at Green Haven in 1979 and the older inmates gave us reefer to congratulate us for obtaining our GEDs. I did not attend church that often but I prayed every night. After eighteen months in Green Haven I saw a great deal of corruption. A few months after I was transferred to the Fishkill Correctional Facility; I recall back in Green Haven a female C.O. was killed and her body dumped in the dumpster and was taken out of the prison walls with the garbage. If it was that easy for alive or dead body to leave the prison many inmates would have used that exit. The inmate they charged with her murder made the perfect fall guy. He was serving life for a very bad crime and he had little to no support from family and friends and he was considered bugged out by inmates and staff so he made the perfect fall guy to blame the killing on. I made this observation because while in Green Haven back in 1978 there was this so called jail break. These two inmates was supposed to be escorted to a doctor's appointment outside of the prison; but the truth of the matter was that they paid to be taken to the hotel a few miles from the prison to meet their girlfriends and they eased away from the officers who was monitoring them. However a cover up story was created by the correction officers that the prison van had gotten hijacked by one of the inmate's people and they broke the jaw of one of the escorting correction officers. Everyone that was in Green Haven prison knew that it was a lie and that what really happened was those two guys sneaked away from the hotel. How is this related to the fall guy is that after the so-called jail break there was an investigation in Green Haven and while working in the mess hall where the C.Os involved in the escape worked this new cook came to work cooking food for the inmate population in the mess hall and he was offering inmates chicken and steaks if they would tell him about the escape. One inmate told one of the correction officers involved in the escape who worked in the mess hall and he and another C.O. jacked up the cook and marched him to the door of the prison and informed him that if he came back into Green Haven he would never make it out alive. It is said, that the lady C.O. who was "so called" killed by the perfect fall guy inmate, father worked in the intelligence department for corrections in Albany and that she was there trying to find out about what happened with the escape of the two inmates. Most inmates believe she got to close and was killed by someone other than the perfect fall guy inmate who was found guilty of her death. The death of this female C.O. happened in 1979, a few months after I was transferred to Fishkill Correctional Facility. The prison system was very corrupt in the 1970s and while at Fishkill I purchased my marijuana from a C.O. and my favorite C.O. told me he did not mind if we smoked reefer it's the wine that he will not have because wine made inmates violent, so for just about all of my 7 ½ years of incarceration, I smoked reefer throughout my bid. While at Fishkill, PeeWee and I had a basketball team called "Like It Rough" and our game chant was "how you like it, rough, how you like it, rough, rough as what, sandpaper, who are we gangsters, what are we going to do, win,!" With that name we won 37 straight games and everyone wanted to beat "Like it Rough " from 1980 to 1982 in Fishkill. My point guard was Curry he was from Harlem and he was a gangster from the heart. Curry and his brother Kevin were gangsters and they both died the death of gangsters. Curry was shot in the head on 7th avenue and 141st street in 1985 and Kevin was gunned down on McCombs Dam Bridge in 1987.

In June of 1980 I was called to the Chaplain's office which is a call that all inmates dread receiving. I was told by the Chaplain that my brother Kaye died. I learned from my mother that Kaye had died from a heroin overdose on the roof of a building in 123rd street. I learned that his good friend Steve paid for the funeral service. I promised myself that I would come home and get paid that much more because of my brother, Kaye's death from heroin. I have often wondered why so many of my siblings and community members made such poor choices like using drugs or selling drugs. I had my brother Kaye, Greg, Pee Nut and Haroldine as well as my sister's Rossetta, Anne and Sandra were all strung out on drugs and all died of drug related deaths throughout the years; except Pee Nut. It took Pee Nut 45 years of using heroine to Crack Cocaine and to finally break free of drug addiction in the year 2012. Then there was the Maybrey family, June Bug, Jackie, Ronald, Doug and Little Greg that lived in 260 West 122nd street, all died from drug related deaths. There was one mother whose only child died from an overdose of heroin wiping out her whole family in 1969. Harlem has so many drug related deaths and I often wondered why? However my mind was made up, when I got out I was going to live a gangster life and get paid.

In August of 1980 a month before my Parole hearing I was playing chess with this chump from Brooklyn and we both did not like each other but for some reason I was playing him chess and we started talking jive to each other and the next thing I knew the both of us was in the bath room fighting and I knocked him out. The C.O. was running to the bath room as I came out of it, and I ended up in the hole for about three days. They let me go early because he did not tell what happened in the bathroom. In September 1980, I went to the Parole Board hearing and when it came my turn to see the Parole Board they announced "there has been a change in the order, the person James White will be going in Larry Coldwell's slot and Coldwell will be going in James White's slot". It just so happen that James White was the chump I knocked out in the bathroom in August and he came out with a parole date and when I went in his slot I was hit with 18 months and instructed to see a psychiatrist if I hope to one day be paroled. The more I thought about it, I realized that the Parole Board gave that chump a Parole date with the understanding that he tell them what happened in that bath room. You see, all of my four years up state I made sure I did not have too many fights because I knew it would be used against me as being violent. So here I was with, an 18 months Parole Board hit; I stayed in bed for about a week after going to the Parole Board hearing that day. As for James White, about 6 months after he went back to Brooklyn he was on the news for sticking up a store with some other guys and he was snitching on them. I begin seeing a psychiatrist for six months and he helped me to understand where my anger came from, which was the hate I had for my father for not being in my life when I felt I needed him. I was never given any diagnosis for mental health ailment, and the psychiatrist was a nice person.

CHAPTER 10

In May of 1982 I was paroled and my homeboy Curry was home. I was given $5,000 to buy a van to start working as a driver for a messenger service down town by homeboys Buddy and his nephew. I moved in with my young girl Cynt who had a one bed room apartment on 129 St. and St. Nicholas avenue. I would smoke reefer while working and when I was sent on an assignment to deliver the mail I would forget where in the hell I parked my van. The job did not pay much at all. I was paid $45 a week and I would always have to ask some of the guys in the block that were hustling to let me hold some money to buy gas. Cynt and I would go to church on Sunday because she was raised as a Christian and I was a born again UNCOMMITED Christian. One day in 1982 while waiting for my homeboy Green Tape to come to the block; I begin talking to my childhood friend Apple Jack as we waited for homeboy to come to the block so that we could ask him for some financial help. Apple Jack and I was talking about when we were kids and how we would steal his mother's sweet potato pies off her window that she placed there to cool off. Apple Jack's mother we called her Ma Gray, made some very good sweet potato pies. Well while we waited on homeboy, Apple Jack said Love come with me to Harlem Hospital so I can get a penicillin shot because I have the Claps. Before I could respond to him, I heard something in a still quiet voice like that voice which spoke to me about paying for my behavior. The voice clearly said "Larry Apple Jack is a stick up kid and he is subject to get killed at any time." I said to Apple Jack, I am going to wait on homeboy. We continued to talk as we stood there on 7th avenue in front of the Walton building on the corner of 122nd street on 7th avenue down town side of the avenue. Apple Jack said again come on Love and go with me to Harlem hospital and we can see homeboy Buddy when we come back. Again that quiet voice said "Larry he is a stick up kid and he might get killed at any moment." Again I responded to him, no man, I want to wait for Buddy. Apple Jack asked me a third time to go with him to Harlem Hospital to get a penicillin shot. This time something said to me "Larry he was in jail for 12 months and he has been home for 2 months hanging with Buddy, so he has not stuck up anyone in 14 months so you can go with him." I said okay, lets go. Apple Jack and I walked uptown heading to Harlem Hospital from our block and by the time we got to 127th street and Lenox avenue a guy stepped out of the shadows of a building and gunned Apple Jack down by way of shooting him in the back and I was shot in the arm by accident. As I took off running and looked back to see what had happened, I saw Apple Jack laying face down on the side walk. I ran into the back yard to get away because I did not know who the shooter was nor how many there was just like in the movies when there is a shooting everyone closed their windows and everything gets quiet and that's how it was with me in the back yard watching people looking at me and closing their windows. I called out for them to call the police but no one responded to my cry for help at all. I was told that Apple Jack got killed because he stuck this guy up a few years ago. From that day on I stayed strapped and ready to defend. I did not go to the hospital because I had just came home for manslaughter and if I was connected to the incident I could have gotten violated for association with an ex-felon. I was fortunate the bullet went in and out of my arm, so I had my brother in-law who was a Medic in the Army fixed me up and since I was living the gangster life of a James Cagney character; he would never go to the hospital in one of his movies when shot nor could I, as a American Black gangster.

In October of 1982 I stop working as a van owner messenger, and I began selling drugs with this guy name Black in my block. The reason I start working with Black is because I was off the seen for eight years and they were now sealing $20 a bag of P Funk and the bags were the same size as the $2 bags of heroin we sold before I went to prison. So I had to learn what this $20 bag of P Funk was all about. The one thing for sure about the $20 P Funk was that you could make just as much money a day as those $75 quarter bags of scrambled heroin those 116th St. guys made. In fact 122nd St. was the only block sealing P Funk in Harlem and P Funk was as close to pure heroin one could get for street sale. Black went off to live in California out of nowhere leaving me with no work, so I then, hooked up with Skiter and some Bronx gangsters that knew me from the time I was in prison. I introduced my own brand of P Funk in 122nd St. and I was getting paid from Brown Tape known as P-Funk being sold in 122nd street. In 1983 my young girl and I had our first child name Levesa Mahogany Coldwell. I was so proud of my first child and she is the first girl I ever promised I would be right back and kept my promise to. I would have Levesa with me almost everywhere I went including in church on Sundays. Levesa's mother and I married in 1984 and lived in a $50,000 Coop in the Bronx. Money was coming in and I had about fifteen people on my payroll a week who were happy and living large. Life as a Black gangster brought in $10,000 dollars a day for me and the more I made the more my white lawyer demanded whenever I was arrested. Money came and money took wings and left just as fast as it came. Pee Wee came home in 1984 and I gave him $5000.00 and he hooked up with me. I had women whom I was cheating on my wife and the mother of my child with giving them money as well and driving a New Yorker car.

Yet I found no happiness in the gangster life at all, because I could clearly see that I was causing more pain to my own people no matter how many free bus rides to Action Park or block parties I gave or turkey's I passed out on Thanksgiving, or the many kids sneakers and shoes I brought for them to start the school year. Skiter would often ask me "Love why you are not happy with all the money we're making?" I could not tell him that when I'm in a corner store and a kid comes in to cash in soda cans and the creep foreign store owner refuses to accept the cans I get mad as hell because as a little boy my brother Kaye and I depended on the corner store accepting our cans and giving us the nickels for the cans. I would go off and break up the store leading to being arrested. In 1985 there was this song out called "Black Butterfly" and I would play it often in Aleas's restaurant in the Bronx , where our crew ate and hung out. Some of the words in the song are "Black butterfly sail across the waters and tell your sons and daughters of the trouble you've seen." Skiter could not understand why I liked that song. It's because I did not like the gangster life I was now living and the harm I helped cause among my own people. When it came to Skiter and my view on how we made our living I felt like Super-Fly talking to his partner and friend Fast Eddie. Super-Fly just wanted to make enough money to get out of the Ghetto and Fast Eddie wanted to reign as King of the Ghetto. My goal in the Gangster life was to make enough money to purchase my own home, own a business fully paid for and save up 500, 000.00 and then get the hell out of the game. It seem like every time I got close to my goal things came up where I would take a big financial lost causing me to keep trying to get to my goal just like Super Fly in the movie.

My beloved Levesa caught a very bad ear infection one day in early 1984 while we were living on 129 street and St. Nicholas avenue, and for about a week the doctors kept breaking her fever and sending her home every day, until I got tired of it and demanded that they keep her in the hospital until she was well. The doctors were playing on the fact that we were first time parents and did not want to leave Levesa in the hospital no more than we had to. Her medical condition only got worse, and so I had to make Mount Sinai keep her the last time we took her to the hospital for the ear infection. Levesa was admitted and was in the hospital for seventeen days. Levesa had a room where her mother would sleep over and her grandmother would stay with her. I would be in and out of the hospital throughout everyday however, I did not spend the night because I could not smoke reefer in the hospital room. I also used this opportunity to cheat on my wife while she is in the hospital with our daughter. So one day a quiet voice in my head said to me "you better spend the night with your daughter before you wish you had." This was my third time experiencing this quiet voice or was it the same voice that night in 6, block when I saw the writing on the wall. Mind you I was an America Black gangster selling drugs to my people and going to church with my wife and daughter on Sundays. I followed the quiet advice in my head and on the 15th night of Levesa being in the hospital with a very bad ear infection drifting away, I sent her mother home and I spent the night with her and did not experience an urge to smoke reefer. There, my ten months old first born daughter lied there fading away. She could not hold food in her and she looked like a sick chicken drying up day by day. For fifteen days, the first thing the nurse would do was to look at Levesa's bowel movement to see if her bowels were holding together and that it was not rancid. So as I look at my only child hooked up to an IV feeder and oxygen machine with a plastic diaper on; that quite voice instructed me to take the IV and oxygen down and place it on her bed so that I could lay Levesa on the sleeping cart that I was to sleep on so that I could pray over her while on my knees. Again I was out there running the streets and tonight here I was with a gun on my hip and reefer in my pocket while I'm on my knees praying to God in the name of Jesus Christ to heal my child. After praying over Levesa I gently placed her back on her bed and readjusted the IV and oxygen and we both slept. The next morning the nurse came in and did as she had done for the past fifteen days. She looked at Levesa's bowel movement to see if it had jelled and the nurse cried out "Oh my God her bowels kept." From that minute forward Levesa was well and we were able to take her home on the 17th day of being in the hospital. I did not give the prayer much thought after taking Lavesa home from the hospital, but I knew it had an impact on Levesa's health.

Here I am patrolling my block early one Wednesday morning when this garbage truck was intentionally tearing down our basketball rim that we had Mr. Buddy hook up to the light pole for us to play ball when we have a chance to play. My brother Greg was a pimp from 42nd street and in the 70's he would bring white girls uptown with him. This morning he came to see me and here I was arguing with the garbage man in the block in front of building 238, who was drunk and tearing down our rim for no reason. Greg pushed the chump and before he could hit him the guy jumped in his truck and came back with the police. I told Greg to be cool and let me handle it. Greg and I was standing in the street in front of building 238 when two policemen and the garbage man approached us and as I spoke to the police Greg took off running straight down the middle of the street with five O (police) hot on his heels heading to 7th avenue. Greg ran down to 7th avenue and turned down 7th avenue to 121st street he then ran up 121st street from 7th avenue and towards 8th avenue he cut through the alley near building 223, backyard. He came out the alley between building 236 and 238 back into 122nd street right where I was standing with Five 0 (police) hot on his heels. I had to laugh and it was funny until the police caught him and bust his head open for no reason. I was mad as hell at the police for hitting Greg just because he ran. Both of us were arrested that morning and we beat the case because of physical abuse from the officer that hit Greg in his head just because he ran as well as about $30,000.00 to my attorney for me and Greg. Greg was still a dust head and that run he took was straight out of a dust head page when he ran straight back across from where he took off from. That case cost me thirty thousand dollars because of our arrest records and the greedy attorney I had. My lawyer beat the case on the police abuse of Greg. Life as an American Black gangster continued to bring in lots of cash. I was still pulling down ten thousand a day. However most of it did not go into my pocket once I let my Connect know that I had ninety thousand saved up. The quality of the work began to get weaker and the cost for the package rose higher. Between my lawyer, payrol and hits I took it seemed like my money had taken wings and flew away. I tried to buy a few buildings on 122nd street and got cheated out of my money. I brought Mr. Layfields candy store on the corner of 122nd and 7th avenue for thirty five thousand dollars and had it fixed up for another ten thousand. I was lead to believe I was buying the store and the abandoned building. A year later I learned that the city owned the building and the store. I was fooled by Mr. Layfield and his realtor because I trusted Mr. Layfield as a kid and always respected him. I also did not think he had the nerve to try and play me. It was easy for him to play me because I was on a merry go round as a Black Gangster and could not stop the merry go round to take time out to check all the paper work as well as all that reefer in my head would not allow me to understand it and those two old fools knew it. They played me out and I could have punished the both of them with no problem, but again that quiet voice in my head told me to "don't go after them". Whenever I thought of setting a trap for them the quiet voice would say 'don't do it." So I let those two old fools get away with cheating me out of my store and building. On October 7th, 1985 while walking to my car that was parked on 123rd street between 7th and 8th avenue in the middle of the block just as I left my store my Parole Officer and Five O (police) jumped out on me and illegally searched me and found a box cutter on me which I told them was used for cutting paper in my store. The Parole Officer violated me there on the spot for the box cutter and I was again in the prison system only this time it was for an illegal stop and search which the Parole Officer and police had no right to stop me without probable cause. I was sent back to Green Heaven where I received my GED in 1979. It was there when I found myself back in Green heaven, that I decided I had enough of smoking reefer so I stopped in spite of all the reefer around me and offered to me there. That quite voice in my head spoke to me again one night and said "Larry in order for you to be alright the crew will be arrested and a homeboy from the crew will die and then you will be alright." About five months of my violation the news came in about March of 1987, that Skiter, Merce, Yakie, Country Bones and Tom were arrested and that homeboy Bunny got killed. I was shocked when I heard the news because it was the clear confirmation of that quiet voice and warning it gave me about five months prior to what went down. The crew was arrested for a body where some stick up kids in the Bronx went to rob this cocaine spot and Skiter's wife was visiting her home girl who was the girlfriend of the guy who owned the cocaine spot. It's said that the stick up kids caught the two ladies going into the building and tried to get the guy to open the door so that they could rob him. When the guy would not open the door to the spot they started beating up the two girls in the hall to get him to open the door and so the guy in the spot began shooting through the door at the stick up kids. Because of the guy shooting from behind the closed door the stick up kids said "man shoot them bitches in the head and let's get the hell out of here." So both ladies were shot in the head and left in the hallway for dead. I know that the guy in the apartment could not have open that door because those guys knew the law of the street and as stick up kids they would have killed everyone caught in that apartment to cover up their identity and to offset any street justice. Well miraculously the two mothers survived with little brain trauma. My crew was charged for this case and placed on Riker's Island, and I was in the Heave for an unfair violation.

CHAPTER 11

So here I am in Green Haven sentenced to serve eighteen months for an illegal arrest and with five months into my sentence when my gangster life seemed to be coming to an end.

My wife and daughter would visit often and I had my laundry mat girl visiting and this sister from the Bronx visit. These two women were some of the women I so freely cheated on my wife with. The one from the Bronx was more of a political connection; she was the god-daughter of the Godfather of Boston Road and dating her put me in a good political position with the Boston road gangsters. She was very smart and devious. One day after we had sex she took and wiped herself clean of our semen with her pantyhose and placed it in my gym bag while I was in the shower. Just as faith would have it, I went home with my gym bag and as I entered our two bedroom Coop in Fordham Hills my wife had the dirty clothes separated on the living room floor preparing to do the laundry and me knowing that my gym cloths needed cleaning I dropped the bag near the laundry and went into the bedroom. In about five minutes my wife came in with the Bronx girls panty whose in her hand asking "whose is this" and I tried to flag it off by telling her "it's Skiter's daughter's"; because she know that Skiter and I was suppose to be playing basketball against a team of guys from 116th street in Harlem. So I took a shower at his house and must have picked up his daughters under clothes by accident. Now his daughters are twelve and eleven years old at the time. My wife showed me all the semen stains on the panty whose and said "these ain't no little girl stains." At this point I snatched them from her and went to the garbage dump to throw them away. But in my mind I was thinking "that dirty bitch she did that intentionally and was probably waiting for me to return to her after fighting with my wife." One thing I can say is that I was a no good cheating dog and had a good women who I treated so unfairly. No matter how much I cheated I would never allow anyone to have a baby outside of my marriage and I never ever met anyone that I thought for a minute to leave my wife for.

One night while serving the 18 months violation in Green Haven D block, I had this strange dream. My body was laying flat on my back and yet, my spirit was sitting up in the middle of my flat body, and my spirit was rebuking this image that was dressed like Dark Vader on the outside of the cell bars trying to pull my body to it and my spirit was sitting up saying "I rebuke you in the name of Jesus Christ." I have never experienced this again in my life, but it was so strange because I was very much aware of what was happening yet, my body was laying there asleep. While serving the violation a year to the date that the Parole office and five O (police) arrested me, my lawyer Ed Wilford and Big H that grew up on 119th street, called me to the phone while in Green Haven and the Department of Parole offered to release me that day if I would agree not to sue them. I beat the violation and I agreed not to sue the department of corrections for illegally stopping me for no reason while walking to my car, because I wanted to get the hell out of jail. I was released on October 7th 1986 at about 3pm around the same time I was arrested. Attorney Big H from 144th street father picked me up from Green Heaven in his 1986 Cadillac causing me to look like a true Gangster that has just legally beat the parole system and coming home in Gangster style. I came back on the scene and all of my P funk customers were hooked on crack cocaine. I had grown tired of the drug game by this time and being a Black American Gangster did not crank up to be anything I thought it would be; but then again, I don't know what the hell I thought it would be. What I did know for sure is that from 1984 through 1987, I did not like what crack was doing to my people. I had one P funk customer who used to sell me gold jewelry in 1983-85, and now she tried to sell me baby clothes due to her addiction to Crack. Crack was taking my people to the lowest ghetto level ever and I wanted no part of it and was sick of the Gangster life. I went from drinking Moet and Taittinger champagne with Von Zip and others to drinking Cordon Negro, which is $4.00, bottles of cheap champagne.

Well in 1987 the Feds came down hard on the Harlem, Bronx, Brooklyn and Queens Black and Spanish drug dealers and began rounding up crews from all boroughs. I knew they were coming for me in spite of my Bronx crew being in jail since 1986. I thought about taking it on the lamb but I could not leave my wife and daughter behind and I could not live on the lamb with them nor without them.

All spring of 1987 I waited for the feds to come knocking on my door at any time, and on July 7th, 1987 while home with my Levesa because her mother had gone to a doctor's appointment at around 11AM, that expected knock came just as I expected it would. Knock, knock I said "who is it" Open up its the FBI, I said "I will come peacefully if you allow me to call my sister to come pick up my daughter." The Feds said "okay" call her and open up." I called my sister Carolyn whom I had made earlier arrangements with because Carolyn lived on 175th street and the Grand Concourse and I lived in Fordham Hills on 207th street and Webb Avenue near the Grand Concourse. My sister arrived about twenty minutes later and the feds gave her my Levesa. It was not until a week after my arrest that my wife told me she was pregnant. I knew we were headed for troublesome times and the times would not be good for a pregnant women. When Cynt was pregnant with Levesa , I did my best to keep things cool and calm around her during her pregnancy because I felt and believed that the psychological stress on a pregnant women, impacts the unborn fetus psychologically. The Feds put me under arrest from my Co-op apartment and drove me from Fordham Hills on Fordham Road to Harlem down 7th avenue past 122nd street. I saw Steve sitting in our regular meeting spot where we would stand around drinking our $4.00 dollar champagne for hours talking jive. When I arrived at the federal holding center downtown at Farley Square and housed on the seventh floor there was all of our Bronx crew Sketer, Volvo Bob, Big Bones, Merc, Yankee, Elsun, Fat Boy and Uncle Harvey and a few others from our crew. I was told that they also had a few women from our crew that was already out on bail. They also had this guy named Mike that was my lieutenant there and all the evidence they had against me was evidence they got from arresting Mike who was serving fifteen years from an arrest on 122nd street. All the evidence that they had on him was placed on me because they had nothing on me. Mike was now here in **MCC** Metropoliten Correctional Center with the crew which he did not know any of them. I kept Mike on 122nd street and would never bring him to the Bronx. The only person from 122nd street I ever brought to the Bronx was Charlie Bee, and he was not able to run with the Bronx Gangsters. I was advised to leave Charlie Bee in Harlem and keep him out of the Bronx. Most guys from Harlem in the 1980s made good drug dealers but they did not have what it took to run with the gangsters from the Bronx. There were only three Harlem-mites that I knew of who were able to run with the Bronx gangsters and they were Buddy from 116th street, Skiter from Convent Avenue and Larry Love from 122nd street. Many Harlem-mites have tried running in the Bronx but the only three survived are the names I shared and out of the three Skiter and Buddy ended up with life without any chance of parole. That federal charge of 848 is a charge of life without any chance of parole, and it is a very unfair sentence because the drugs they had was brought to them by white people who did not face life without any chance of parole. Well on December 24, 1987 my wife gave birth to a set of five months premature twin girls. Things were very hard on my wife and as she learned of my many infidelities. She shared a lot of her emotions with the twins while pregnant. Cynt would not let me talk to Levesa on the phone, and when she sent me clothes for court she would cut the crotch of my pants out and all those negative thoughts she had of me and my cheating dog ways were transferred to the twins she was carrying. My twins and I have not been able to share the kind of father and daughter relationship that Levesa and I share, even now that they are grown women. Please know that I don't blame my former wife for anything, I just wish it never happened the way it did, and my hope is that my twins will one day find it in their hearts to forgive me for whatever wrong they feel that I have committed, so that they can learn to truly love someone.

Well here I was with all the American White, Black and Latino gangsters of the seventies and eighties. The White gangsters from Hell's kitchen to Little Italy took a liking to our crew and yielded to us running the joint. Here I sit in MCC facing charges of 848, life without parole for organized crime and drug possession. All of us had the same three counts. So there I sat at 35 years old with a wife and three daughters needing me desperately and there's nothing I could do about it. One day the Feds took me to a back office to get me to snitch on everyone. When I finished giving them a piece of my mind they never took me to that back office again. I always knew that there would be a day of reckoning for my behavior and I counted the cost and accepted the reality that I might have to pay with my life or freedom. However I was tired of always finding myself behind the eight ball and facing lots of years in prison. It was at this point that I knew that I had to change my life for the better. We were in the early legal stages of the case but growing up in the street life we were taught that when the Feds come to get you that means they have all the goods they needed and the jig (game) is up. I had no idea what the outcome of this situation would be but I knew we were not going to win this case at trial. I tried to get Skiter to understand that but he believed that we were going to beat the case. It was around January 1987 when I was in the cell thinking about all of myself destructive behavior and what was the root cause of it when I realized that I was mad as hell at my father Moies for not being in my life when I needed him as a little child; just as the psychiatrist said when I was seeing him in Fishkill after I was denied Parole in October 1980 and ordered to see a psychiatrist if I hope to be paroled after my 18 months Parole hit was up.

CHAPTER 12

I realized that my ability to be as mean as I needed to be in the street life stemmed from my anger bottled up in me from my father who did not get along with my mother and only came around when he was drunk and would fight my mother for what reasons I never could understand. The more I thought about it the more I realized that I had to forgive my father for not being in my life when I needed him as a frightened child living in Harlem. It was at that time I decided to forgive him for not being there when I needed him the most; mind you he had been dead since 1970 but in 1987 when I forgave him from my heart I felt as if a pack of bricks were taken off my back and I felt free of all the hate and anger that fueled me to become that crazy nigger on 122nd street, that everyone knew not to mess with. From that day forward my life began to take a paradigm shift and I heard that quiet voice in my head and it said to me "Larry you're making a wreck of your life you need to turn your life over to a power greater than yourself." It was not until about ten years later, that I learned that was an NA saying, which I had never heard until that day while sitting in the cell there in the Federal holding pin. So I honestly surrendered my life to God in the holy name of Jesus Christ, by not just dropping my guns and putting my hands up in the air in surrender; I truly surrendered by throwing down my guns and foolish thinking ways and walking out backwards with my hands held high in the air, it was a total surrender, which I was suppose to have done that day back there on Riker's Island when I accepted Jesus Christ as my Lord and Savior half heartedly. I made no deals with my God when I surrendered, all I asked for God to do was walk with me throughout this prison sentence and life journey, as I had no ideal just how long it would be.

The trial judge Robert Ward liked everyone on our case and he called us his boys, and he also told me one day "Larry, you're a free spirit." Our trial lasted six months at four days a week of trial and the jury deliberated for nineteen days before they came back with a verdict of guilty. In July of 1988 everyone except Mike was convicted of organized crime and the sale of heroin. Mike was sent back up state to finish his 15 years prison sentence. We all beat the 848 count except Skiter, he was convicted with the 848 life without parole count. Upon sentencing the judge told all of us "if things don't go well on your appeal write me a rule 35 motion and I will consider it". A rule 35 motion under the old law is just a plea to the judge asking for mercy and anyone could write it for you or you can write it yourself. Everyone was fixed on beating the Feds on appeal but again I knew we did not stand a chance. At trial the Feds said I made a statement which I don't recall making. The Feds said that I said "when this is over I'm going straight," I don't remember saying that but it damn sure sounded like a good idea to me. The two women got suspended sentences and Mike and another brother beat the case because they truly were not a part of our crew. One good thing about our trial was that this guy was serving 25 years to life for a murder he did not commit and because of our trial the truth came out that he was not the potato chip hit man. It's said that a guy was walking down 7th avenue eating a bag of potato chips and when he reached his target he came out of the bag of chips with a 38 revolver and shot his target. The evidence came out that it was someone on trial with Skiter's crew who was the potato chips hit man. So the guy had been in prison serving

25 years to life for about six years and within a few weeks he was exonerated for the charge of murder and out of prison before our trial ended. After sentencing in September of 1988, I was sent to Lompoc Maximum Prison, in Lompoc California to begin serving fifteen years for organized crime and fifteen years for selling drugs. Both charges ran consecutive meaning I had a 30 years federal prison sentence; others received 25 years and some 35 years and Skiter got an 848 life without parole sentence at 38 years old. I was serving time as a total surrendered born again Christian learning about God from a Christian perspective with no focus on anything other than learning about this guy called Jesus Christ whom I had accepted there on Riker's Island in the 1970s. While at Lompoc this made guy would call me into his cell to try and get me to join his crime syndicate and I would tell him "I quit the gangster life." I also had this Muslim brother who would always solicit me to join Islam, and I would tell him that I wanted that "old time religion that was good enough for my mother." At Lompoc every six months they would call me to a conduct committee meeting and I would ask to be transferred to Lewisburg Prison in Pennsylvania which was closer to New York City and my family. At this hearing they would always tell me that I'm not eligible for parole until 2007. One time I asked to be transferred to Lewisburg because I had been behaving and they said to me "your only doing yourself a favor by behaving." I thought what he said made a lot of sense to me. I spent eighteen months at Lompoc Penitentiary and in 1990 I was transferred to Lewisburg. When I was in Lompoc Prison and trying to get transferred to Lewisburg the guys at Lompoc that was from the East Cost, would tell me war stories about Lewisburg to scare me out of going there and I would tell them "I did not care if King Kong was at Lewisburg, it was the closest I could get to my family and that's all I needed." When people knew that they were going to Lewisburg they would psych themselves into the mindset "If a nigger violate me I'm going to kill him." I did not

WHO RAISED HIM

take on the mindset because I was sold out on walking with God in the holy name of Jesus Christ and I did not anticipate having any problems because I knew if I stayed clear of the drugs, alcohol, gambling and gay guys all would be well. My first week in the Burg (Lewisburg) they served fried chicken for the first time and this guy stabbed another guy to death in the mess hall because the guy who was killed had been sitting in the guy's seat in the mess hall who had been sitting in that seat for the past twenty years and the other guy refused to give the seat back to the twenty year sitter who sat in that seat for 20 years. The three years I served in Lewisburg had many murders and the strange thing about it was that almost all of them the person that got killed or did the killing had less than one year to go before they were to be released from prison. There was one killing over some bread, one over the TV commercial and one was a suicide by way of provoking someone to take him out of his misery of having to serve 30 years under the new law, which means he had to do something like 24 years before he could get out. Death in Lewisburg was real strange to me. It was at Lewisburg that I began to do some soul searching as I began to take a honest look within myself and come to terms with what I discovered about myself; just as Michael Jackson song "Man in the Mirror" suggested we do.

One day while waiting on sick call line to get pills for a cold I was standing in front of "A" block. "A" block housed the most aggressive inmates in Lewisburg and I was just observing them and I noticed that I was nothing like them for some of them had killed and would kill just because they could. I was so happy to receive this revelation. I wrote to my wife's mother and apologized to her for thinking I was so bad. My wife and children came to see me in Lewisburg and I would have a very hard time connecting with my twins during the visiting hours; we seem to just not get along at all. Levesa and I would play and laugh throughout the visit but my twins would never laugh with me. My visits were my hardest days while incarcerated because my twins and I could not connect as father and daughters. While self reflecting one day, I realized that I was committed to a bunch of guys that I would put my life on the line for if it came down to it; and it could have very well came a time when those same guys might come for my life because in the world of gangster hood the only real loyalty a gangster has is to the mighty dollar; anything and anyone else was open game. So here I was loyal to some people to the point of death if it came down to it and yet I was so disloyal to my wife who might have given her life for mine if it came down to it. I realized that I had misguided loyalty and was loyal to the point of possible death to the wrong people. From that day forward I made up my mind that I would never again allow myself to place my loyalty in the wrong place again. From that day forward my loyalty to the point of death was to my former wife and children. My former wife would come up to visit for the weekend and they would stay with a white Christian family from the Mennonite Faith. They took very good care of the inmates families who came to visit for the weekend. In 1991 Skiter, Fats and El were in Lewisburg with me. I spent most of my social time interacting with the church brothers. However from time to time El and I would talk about our appeal and Judge Wards promise to look out for us. We asked around if anyone had ever been promised by a Federal Judge and it was unheard of. As a Christian I embraced it as divine intervention on our behalf. So we would all say "we hope Judge Ward did not die before acting on our rule 35 motion" In 1992 we lost our federal appeal. The United States Supreme Court said we had issues of concern but they were not enough to overturn the conviction. A few months later we all received a letter from Judge Ward to submit a rule 35 motion to him; which is just an appeal to the judge to have mercy and reconsider the sentence. I wrote my rule 35 motion myself and explain to the Judge that my brother Johnny Kaye overdosed and died from heroin in 1980, my sister Anne died from alcohol in 1990 and my brothers Greg, Pee Nut, Haroldine as well as my sisters Rosetta, Sain and Bay were currently strung out on heroin and crack from the 70's untill the date of my motion and how I had been shot two different times as well as served over twelve years in and out of jails and institutions; and that I was just as much a victim as anyone else. As we waited through the years for the Judge's response to our rule 35 motion he would send word to us by one of the sisters on our case "tell the boys, I have not forgotten about them". One day while in Lewisburg El and I was talking about the criminal life we grew up living and I told him that "snitching is a part of the drug game, it's not a part that I would ever play." But when it happens I am not surprised by the person who turns snitch. You see if we are supplying our own sisters and brothers drugs by proxy then why should there be any loyalty to a game that victimize your own people. In our trial we had a number of made guys that snitched on us and lied about what they were telling about us. That's why Skiter got hit so hard at trial because a cousin of a number of guys in our crew snitched on Skiter and he lied as well. El had a difficult time coming to terms with my view on snitching but him and I often found ourselves discussing the pros and cons of the American Black Gangster life and we both agreed that it was time to put it behind us. One day Skiter and I were talking while watching a baseball game in the yard and he asked me was I really getting out of the game for good and when I assured him that I was in the name of Jesus Christ he could not understand why anyone would quit the life. He walked away from me shaking his head and I knew then and there that I had let that losing life pass me by in the holy name of Jesus Christ. I never called him back and we hardly spoke much after that July 1992. One day while working in the Factory industry that I was told only Senators and Congress members could own stock in the Federal Prison system Factory, where we made cables for fighter jets. One day I asked the C.O. about a new medium security prison facility that opened up near Lewisburg. I needed the address for my sister. The C.O. said "well, Coldwell why do you ask about this prison?" and I responded "my sister Carolyn told me my nephew was sentenced to it." The C.O. then responded "well, Coldwell we want to thank you and the Coldwell family". I became high alert and on guard for his next words and he went on to say "for keeping us with a job". I was hurt and wanted to hurt back but as I reflected on what he had just said, there was not a word I could find wrong with this white man's statement. So I just turned and walked away with my head held high and I thought to myself with my head held high that I can't help being in prison this time but if I were to ever get out of prison I would do all I can to put that punk on welfare by staying the hell out of these money making prisons for the white man". I was not mad at what he said I was angry at myself because I knew what he said was true and my brothers and I have been keeping our oppressors employed since our youth and now my nephews are keeping them employed as well. My nephew Mike came through Lewisburg orientation on his way to a medium facility in Pennsylvania. I was able to talk to him from his cell window and he told me how all my nephews were mad at me and when I asked him why he said "because you would not put us down with the drug game". Well here he was speaking to me from Lewisburg prison cell with a ten year prison sentence under the new President Clinton drug law where you have a mandatory 85% of your prison sentence to serve. This is not my nephew whom I asked the C.O. about the new prison near Lewisburg. That was his brother and now Mike is here falling head long into the same trap that caught his brother Troy. My nephews did not grow up serving time in juvenile facilities like my brothers and I did. In fact as I know they had little to no knowledge of the street life at all; and the last time I saw Mike was in April of 1987 one day on the Grand Concourse when he was supposed to be in school and I made him get into my car and took his butt back to his high school on 171st street and Webster Avenue. Now here we met again in June of 1992 with him telling me how they were mad at me for not putting them down in the Gangster life. I just listened to him and said nothing. How could I get him to understand that to bring my sisters child into the dangerous life I was living as an American Black Gangster would put my sister and I relationship in danger because if some harm happened to him like imprisonment or death my sister would hold me responsible because I introduced her child into such a dangerous situation. Also how could I get him to understand that the life I lived was expendable and you only interacted with people that you could afford to lose by way of death or incarceration. Mike was transferred to Ray Brook Correctional Facility which was a medium facility. I continued to look within myself for improvement and I learned that I was not the best looking guy in the world, but I was not the worst looking either. I also learned that I was not the meanest or worst person in the world and that I did not have a heartless spirit to qualify me for such a title. Learning this caused me to like that little lost country boy name Larry Moses a little more. During my time at Lewisburg I met a few interesting people. There was this Jewish guy named Marty who claimed to be the Bondsmen in Atlanta Georgia who bailed out the Civil Rights college students that were demonstrating with the sit inns at the Five and Dime stores in Atlanta during the early stages of the Civil Rights protest. He told me about one of the lead students for the sit in by the name of King who was not related to the Reverend Martin Luther King Jr. He reports that his Bondsmen office was the first one in Atlanta to hire a Black man and that his office was the one who bailed Martin Luther King out when he was arrested for driving without a driver's license; but history has it that President John F. Kennedy made a call to Atlanta and demanded that they release Dr. King. I asked Marty why he supported the Civil Rights Movement and he reported that during the Jim Crow times Jews were targeted just as much as Blacks and that the only difference was that Jewish people just had to change their name and they were able to integrate themselves into the Anglo Saxon dominate culture. Blacks could not integrate themselves into America because they could not change their skin color. I found Marty to be a very interesting person because as a Jew he seemed to command the respect of the Aryan Brotherhood at Lewisburg. I promised Marty that I would tell his story and it has taken me twenty two years to share his story. I think he was serving life in prison for drugs when I met him. Then there was Wally Rice, who Nicky Bonds snitched on. Wally said that Frank James who was Nicky's right hand man would come to visit Nicky for Nicky to hook him up with a Mafia drug connect and that Nicky set them up by telling Frank he could not meet the connect unless Frank brought Wally with him. Frank, brother Jones and Wally were convicted with others as a result of Nicky snitching and setting Wally up, they received an 848 life sentenced without parole. Also Guy Fisher from the Bronx went down when Nicky introduced the snitch game into the American Black Gangster world. I am told that Guy Fisher has earned a PhD and helps young prison inmates earn their G.E.D. I personally feel sorry for all those brothers that are in prison with such an unfair sentence as an 848 life without parole prison sentence. They received the sentence for having five or more separate groups of guys in their crew selling drugs. None of these guys brought any of the drugs into the United States or into their neighborhood for the most part, yet they have no chance of making parole where as Americans caught fighting against the United States during the Iraq conflict can make parole. I met one white guy who had an 848 life without parole his name was Mark R. The law 848 life without parole came from the movie name Little Ceasar played by Edward G. Robinson, his name in the movie was Rico and it stands for Racketeering. The movie was based upon murder, extortion and boot legging. Drug dealers with

848 life without parole for the most part, their only criminal act is being involved in drug selling and not acts displayed in the movie Rico where they got the 848 organized crime concept from. Wally is about 84 years old with poor health and has been in prison since 1982 so with 36 years in the Federal prison, and was let out of Prison due to his poor physical helth. Please tell me if you can, how in the hell does keeping Wally and so many others with 848 sentences in prison for the rest of their lives make our society any better. I say, no it does not. For Wally and all those with 848 Federal prison sentences are victims just as much as those who were purchasing the drugs as well as the fact that 30 years in prison is enough time of someone's life to pay for any and all debts they may have acquired in their negative behavior. I tell you "it is a travesty of justice for the United States of America to keep these people in prison for life, all because they sold drugs to my brothers and sisters and their own family members indirectly. I must also mention the two brothers Victor and Georg Torres, who received 848 sentences at the tender age of thirty years old and have been in prison since we met at MCC in 1987, for selling drugs. I find it a travesty of American justice to incarcerate Blacks and Latino citizens for life from selling drugs that someone white brought to America and I am not talking about the American Mafia. I am saying the American government who took over the Pope fields during the Korean war, where heroin is grown at. Lets look at who the real drug dealers are today.

    I now come to believe that the suppliers of the drug demand from the 1960s till today comes from the United States government who has the power and ability to meet such a tremendous demand for such a large supply of drugs throughout the years. I base this view on the Contro Trial when it was pointed out at Alexander Haig's trial that America was sending guns to South America for an exchange of plane loads of Cocaine. You ask, why, would the government do such a sick and hideous thing like that and I say, they do it and continue to do it as a means of population control to this very date. Population control use to be a big issue here in America and now we don't hear of it as much at all. However, if you think about all the people addicted to drugs be they illegal or pharmacy purchased, you know of, you will learn that most of them lost about 10-30 years of their lives living day to day just to get drugs and others have died or gone to prison for years due to drugs. This is a covert way of controlling the population in line with Population Control.

    Well, my eighteen years state prison sentence for that 1974 body ended in 1992 and my security level was lowered from maximum security to medium security which allowed me to be transferred to a medium correctional facility. In June of 1993 I was transferred to Fairington Correctional Facility in New Jersey at exit 2. I ran into Merc, Hammy Red and Mal at Fairington. As codefendants we would get together in the yard from time to time asking if anyone heard from Judge Ward concerning our rule 35 motion and due to his age we all would respectfully state how we hope he does not die before he made a decision on our motion. I continued to see the committee every six months and all they would talk about is that I would not be eligible for parole until 2007. I recall one conversation I had with some other guys while working in Unicor. Unicor is a factory in the federal Prison system that works the hell out of inmates for 35 cents an hour to build things like cables for Rockets, office furniture, clothes for major clothing companies. The only persons that can own stock in Unicor is politicians, so I am told. Everyone was talking about going home within the next three years and when I was asked when was my expected date to go home I told them "it's going to take a congressional act of congress for me to get out any time soon, and I don't believe congress would act on my behalf; or divine intervention for me to get out of jail any time soon" and divine intervention was my only hope. My soul searching journey came to an end in 1994 and I was all the better for it. I continued to walk hand in hand with my Lord and Savior Jesus Christ. We had a strong church family there and my faith became stronger in the Lord. One day while working in Unicor factory making cable cords for rockets and "F"16 Fighter Jets in November 1994. Mal walked pass my work station and said "Love you heard what happened to Robert and Yak"? Robert and Yak were our two, co-defendants in Ray Brook Correctional Facility in upstate New York. I said "no, I did not", and Mal proceeded to tell me that Robert who was serving 35 years and Yak who was serving 25 years both received a time cut from Judge Robert Ward's ruling on our Rule 35 motion. I got so excited and said "my time cut is in the mail." The C.O. saw me excited and ordered me to calm down and I said to the C.O. "I'm sorry but I got good news and I can't calm down." The C.O. left me there excited. I could not wait until our 4pm work hour was over; let me say that the first time in my life that I had a job and earned a vacation was while working in the industrialized prison complex while serving time in the Lewisburg and Fairington Federal prison system. For working in Unicor you also got something like two months time cut per year off of your prison sentence. Well 4pm was here and it was time to get off working on those cables and as I entered "B" block, I looked at the part of the wall where legal mail notices are posted and there it was Larry Coldwell #747-054 legal mail; keep in mind that this legal mail meant the difference from being in prison until 2007 when the date of this mail is 1994. I was excited but did not want to get my hopes up to high because the system has never been fair to me, so I held my hopes but I was afraid as well. My time was running consecutive; meaning I had a thirty years sentence and the prison system wanted me to serve two thirds of the 30 years prison sentence. I had fifteen years Rico and fifteen years for Conspiracy running concurrently and fifteen years for Narcotics running consecutively giving me a total of 30 years, and I was expected to serve twenty of the thirty years before possible parole due to the fact that I am a Black man who dared to think that he was an American Black Gangster. I had no other reason to expect any other legal mail than the answer from Judge Robert Ward's ruling on my rule 35 motion, and after hearing about Robert and Yak's time cut I reached for my mail with trembling hands because I knew that this letter could change my release from my prison date by ten years or more. As I grabbed the letter I looked for an isolated place to read my mail, as I ripped the envelope open my heart began to beat for joy before I saw the writing of the motion; and as I began to read, it said "counts one and two is reduced to fifteen years to run concurrently" signed by Judge Robert J. Ward. The news energized me a lot and allowed me to dream of freedom in the near future. I continued to walk hand in hand with my Lord and Savior Jesus Christ. The time cut made me eligible for a Parole hearing in 1995, and I began to save things I would need upon my release because I knew that my life had changed and that I was not going in any direction that would jeopardize my freedom. I knew there was no one that would lookout for me like when Buddy and his nephew gave me ten thousand to get up on my feet when I came home in 1982. So here I am in Fairington correctional facility collecting new underwear, socks, boots and federal green clothes to wear when I go home because I knew that my wife had lost everything as well as our fifty thousand Coop in Fordham Hills when purchased and valued at $90,000 when sold. Mind you I did not get one dime of the sale, nor was I informed as to how much she sold it for; however, I heard that she sold it for almost nothing to one of her cousins. She was living in the poorest part of the Bronx in a tenement building infested with rats and roaches when I came home and I hated that neighborhood because it reminded me of when I was a youth living in 122nd St. fighting those rats and roaches at nights before I went to bed. I knew I had work to do to up lift my family when I got out and I knew I would not use any criminal behavior to up life my family and myself. I had also promised myself that I did not know what life choices my daughters would make when they got older, but I promised that I would not be a contributor of any negative choices they would have to choose from. I went to the Parole Board in 1995 for the first time and I truly did not have any high hopes of receiving parole because they have always said that I would have to serve most of my time. The parole officer told me that no one would take a chance that I would not repeat my negative behavior so my chance for parole was hopeless and I was denied parole that day. That is one reason why I worked in Unicor, because if you worked in Unicor you get a time reduction consideration off your prison time not the sentence, but the time meaning if you have a 15 years sentence and you worked in Unicor you can get about 15 months early release from the 10 years that you have to do out of the 15 years, if your case was under the old Law, an our case was dated from 1981 till 1987, which placed our criminal charges under the old law. The new Law came into effect when President Clinton enacted the new prison sentence that you had to serve 85% of your sentence before being eligible for parole. So I began to look forward to the day when I had two thirds of my 15 years prison sentence in for parole.

One day in September of 1995 while sitting in my cell in "B" block on a Sunday waiting for chow to be called, I heard that quiet but clear voice speak to me saying "Larry you must make up your mind right now not when you come from chow or tomorrow; but right now, that you're going to leave that gangster life alone, if you don't you will either die in that life or end up shot up and hurt for life or become an old lonely man in some dark and dirty bar, talking about your waiting on one more customer to see you through." Mind you I have been walking hand in hand with my Lord and Savior Jesus Christ since 1988; so here was this quiet but clear voice telling me to choose to live for God or live a Gangster life in 1995. I promised that quiet voice and myself that I quit the

Gangster life and that I choose to live for Jesus Christ. I guess that quiet voice was for me to be sure that my mind was made up and I'm glad it was. I received a parole date for July, 1996 after serving eight years and nine months. I had little to no real idea how I was going to make a living when I got out of prison, but I knew it was not going to be a life of any criminal behavior. In April of 1996 I was accepted at a halfway house in Brooklyn for ninety days until my July parole date kicked in. While working in Unicor a few days before my transfer to the Brooklyn halfway house this C.O. name **Joe** stopped by my work area and said "Coldwell I heard you're going home soon" and I said "yeah Joe in a few days I'm out of here." He responded "all don't worry about it Coldwell, you will be right back in jail, all your going home and do is sell drugs and kill your own brothers and sisters." The guys sitting with me were mad as hell and said "I told you Love that nigger is racist." Well I reflected on what the correction officer **Joe** who is a white CO, said and I respectfully said in response. "You know Joe, being black and living in New York City I can't rightly say rather I will be back in jail or not because I could be walking down the street and see the police unjustly abusing someone and I say something to the police and could find myself being arrested. However, what I can assure you is that, if coming back to prison means I went home and broke laws that only white people can break and get away with, then I can assure you that I am never coming back to jail again." **Joe** looked at me and winked his left eye and nodded his head (as saying you got it) and walked away. My last act was mailing my box of clothes out of the prison to my wife. The prison normally check the content of all packages that is being mailed out of the facility. However on this day they did not check my box and I'm glad because I knew I would need all the underwear, prison pants, shirts and boots once I got home. In April of 1996 I was transferred to 988 Myrtle Avenue halfway house in Brooklyn. I was there for ninety days and then I was paroled in July. That was the first time

I had ever completed something in my life. My first night home I cleaned up our refrigerator and when my daughters woke up the next day they thought we had a brand new refrigerator. I worked as a custodian at Flimenster House on 22nd street between 11th and 12th avenue and was the best Porter ever. Every dime I was paid went to helping my wife and three daughters. I wore the clothes I mailed out of the Correctional Facility before going to the halfway house. After being home with my family for one year I did not make any impact on my relationship with my twin daughters. There were times when it seemed like things were getting better with us and the next thing I knew our relationship did not show any signs of improvement.

CHAPTER 13

I remember when I first came home in July and walked through 122nd street from 8th avenue down to 7th avenue, and not one person called me by my name or acknowledged me. I was glad that no one living in 122nd street today knew who I was. About a week later I was traveling through the neighborhood and ran into a former customer who wanted to be on my team when I got ready to go to work in the game. I told him that I was a Born Again Christian and that I had no intentions of getting back in that life, and the customer said to me "well you better get the hell out of here because you don't even look the same as you did when you was Larry Love." I was glad when he said that about me not looking the same. I knew that God had freed me of those hate demons that served me in the days when I thought 122nd street was mine. Also I did not see where the people were making money because there were not a lot of people strung out as far as I could see and I was truly happy about that.

One day Steve invited me to a Narcotic Anonymous (NA) celebration at All Saints Church and when I saw all those former drug addicts and crack heads drug free, I was happy for them and when I heard some of the testimonies I was able to identify with them. I heard them talking about how their lives had become unmanageable and how they turned their lives over to a power greater than themselves. I was so surprised to hear that because it was the same thing I went through in 1988, when I surrendered my life to the God of my understanding without ever hearing the NA language in my life. I fell in love with the rooms of Narcotic Anonymous and I wished my brothers and sisters could have found their way into the rooms of N.A. My sister Rosetta died in 1997 of consisted drug abuse. My sister Bay, brother Pee Nut and Haroldine were the only three siblings left still using drugs. I began to hate drugs and its ugly scars it left on my family as well as on me. I would always counsel my daughters of the dangers of using drugs and its damaging impact on the Coldwell family. My mother was happy to see me turn from a life of crime and for the first time in my forty-four years I heard my mother say "I love you Larry". She said it so often when I saw her that I wondered if she was now trying to make up for lost time. The drug usage within my family and community seemed to be winding down as members of my family and community were dying out and it seemed that most of the new generation did not want to be stigmatized as a junkie or crack head. I was so happy about my family and community not indulging in drug usage within our society for whatever reason. In 1998 there was still no improvement with my relationship with my twins. At times when it seemed like I was getting through to them something happened that came and undid all hopes of a possible break through and they would be right back being unresponsive to me. I felt so bad about our relationship and could not understand how to fix it for the life of me. This was the only area of my life that I felt like a failure. My marriage was getting worse as well. I was not able to meet the sexual aspects of my marriage because our love for each other had died while I was serving time.

In October of 1998 my brother in-law Al, my former wife's brother, and I would often have conversations about making better life choices and improving our employment marketability. One day Al challenged me to go with him to register for his second college semester. He wanted me and this other brother to take the college placement exam to see if we qualify for college. Well, I could not pass on a chance to show anyone I communicated with that I was not only smart enough to run a drug ring and not smart enough to qualify for college; so naturally I took the bait. Mind you I had saw a sister name Carolyn who was raising five children single handed and attending college and when I asked her how does she do it she replied "just enroll Larry and do it." That conversation had stuck with me for about two weeks. I was also tired of those minimum wage jobs that I found and lost just as fast as I found them. I knew I would have to return to college if I had any chance of improving my employment marketability. Yes, that's right I said "return to college". While serving six to eighteen years in1980 at Fishkill Correctional Facility I enrolled into Dutchess County College when college degrees were offered to inmates. I did one semester and dropped out after that because I could not study gangsterology and smoke reefer which made me dumber than what I was, and serve out my sentence and learn at Dutchess College. So I dropped out of college and stayed smoked up while serving time and learned all I could about how to be that Black American Gangster.

There I sat, at Mercy College Campus on 92nd street and Amsterdam and Columbus Avenue. The exam took about two hours. I received an answer that evening that I had scored well enough to qualify for enrollment into Mercy College. I was accepted and by the way the other brother was not accepted. I told my wife about it and asked her to sign the paper for me to take out a loan to go to college and she said straight up "NO". When she said it I could not believe her and it took me three months of begging her like Delilah begged Samson for his powerful secret and like Samson she gave in and I enrolled into college in the spring of 1999. Our marriage was coming to its end by this time. My wife would be out late and I had no knowledge where she was or had been. I continued to walk hand in hand with my Savior

Jesus Christ and found myself making NA meetings to fill up my day with something positive. One day in March of 1999, while going to work I said to my wife "everyone in this house who can work should be working to help out". Her reply to that was "you can leave"; I said nothing to that, but something did not sit right with me all that day and when I returned home that Monday in March of 1999 I noticed that the lock on the door had been changed and my key did not work. I said a prayer to myself and then knocked on the door. She opened the door and I noticed all my few things were there by the door packed in two bags. She told me I had to leave and I did not ask why. You see I would have never left on my own but I was relieved when she gave me my walking papers because life with me working minimum wage jobs and going nowhere was taking a toll on me. I also hated living in that ghetto area of 136th street and Willis avenue in the Bronx which brought me back to the life of rats and roaches that I had fought and sold drugs in hopes of escaping to only be brought back to it. As I left the apartment I noticed my 3 daughters were in the twins room with the door closed and they were laughing, as I was being put out. I had not heard that quiet and clear voice in a while but as I was walking out of that building on 136th street and Willis Avenue in the Bronx that voice said "Larry at least you're not in jail." It was a cold and raining Monday night but I walked down to 136th street and Alexander Avenue to where my niece Chyrelle lived with her two sons. Chyrelle gladly took me in for two days. I then moved into a room in my sister Doris apartment at 170th street and 3rd avenue. I was dragged into child support court and the judge tried to make me stop going to school so that I could work more hours to pay child support. I had no problem paying child support and did it before the court said to do it. I remember being in the child support court and for the life of me I could not understand why there were no white families going through child support. The magistrate did all he could to make me feel like dirt and he was very unfair on every ruling. I tried to be a part of my children's lives and the harder I tried the more they pushed me away. I lived with my sister Doris for 18 months. One day in 1999 I had just came from shopping for winter clothes because I had plans to move to Albany, when Pee Wee's sister Joanne who lived around 170th street and 3rd Avenue saw me and asked "Larry what is going on" I told Joanne about my divorce and my plans to move to Albany because section 8 takes years to kick in. Joanne advised me to have my section 8 application upgraded to top priority by telling them I was homeless. Thanks to her and God I had my section 8 voucher within 6 months of talking to her. That's another place where I never saw any white people applying for vouchers as if they don't have divorce problems or homeless problems. This was a new world to me but I was determined to make something positive out of my life no matter what challenges I came face to face with.

I joined Canaan Baptist Church of Christ, in 1999 because I liked how Dr. Wyatt T. Walker the pastor would give you a history of the old Negro Spirituals like the Song "Wade in the Water," Dr. Walker pointed out that when the song was being sung by the slaves they were sending a message to the slaves who was running away from the Slave Master, for them to wade in the Water because the slave catchers were on their trail pursuing them and that they would be safe in the Water where the hound dogs would not be able to catch their scent.

I became a disciple of Canaan Baptist Church of Christ and joined their Prison Ministry in 2001. My goal in Prison Ministry is to put that correction officer in Lewisburg who "thanked me and my family for keeping him and his family with a job by being in jail", on Welfare by sharing to inmates that there is freedom from incarceration through the precious blood of Jesus Christ and that one can make better life choices that does not lead to incarceration. Mind you, that correction office had probably long sense retired I believe; but I am sure that his son is not a correction office because of me being in prison. We minister at Riker's Island on the second Saturday of every month at the Rose M. Singer Center where the females are housed. What moved me was that these young girls seemed like they should have been on a college campus and not there on Riker's Island where some of them are facing a lot of time for murder and robbery. They look so much like Michael Jackson's PYTs. I remember back in the 1970s when very few PYTs were in jail and the only female inmates were your older junkies and prostitutes. We also minister at Eastern Correctional Facility also known as Napanoch which is a 2 hour drive from New York City, where I served 18 months of my 6 to 18 years prison sentence and also where I was baptized at in 1977. The brothers at Napanoch looked just like me and they seem to be most of the population. As we walk through the yard from the entrance which is about a 2 city block walk, we see lots of inmates out in the yard and some watching the same 3 TVs in the bleachers that Pee Wee and I watched while serving 6 to 18 years. Some playing chess by the bleachers and others playing baseball in the open field. When I was in Napanoch back in 1977, it was said that the KKK use to conduct their cross burning sessions there in the yard back in the days, I never saw anything like it nor did I notice any KKK like behavior or attitudes when I was there. However, I saw and heard it loud and clear those 90 days there at Danimore Clinton orientation. I also drive the Canaan Baptist Church of Christ church Van to Riker's Island and Napanoch for our ministry on the days we visited there.

I also liked Pastor Walker's style of preaching because his messages were focused on the application of the struggles of everyday life. He would preach about Jesus Christ and how Jesus wants Black People to stand up for their rights just as Jesus stood up for His. I also joined Canaan because of an older brother called Pop Miller who was on the Pastoral staff at Canaan. He and I became friends in 1997 when he assisted me in officiating my first funeral service for my friend Pee Wee's niece who was very sick and died and her mother Pee Wee's sister, Debbie, asked me to preach her daughter's funeral service. It was my first time ever preaching a funeral service. I have always believed as a Christian that God in the name of Jesus Christ hears His children whether they are ministers or just born again Christians with a willingness to serve others. So, when Debbie asked me to preach her daughter, Nicole's, funeral I did not give it a second thought. However, I was told that I would need a licensed minister to consecrate the body for burial. I did not agree with it but for the sake of peace for Debbie and her family I asked Steve if he knew of anyone and that's when I was introduced to Pop Miller as he was affectionately called by everyone in Canaan Baptist Church of Christ and the Harlem community. Pop consecrated the body and he and I were friends up until the day of his death some 12 years later. I really enjoyed worshiping at Canaan. They had a service once a year when the elders would dress up in overalls and the women would dress in those dresses and head wraps from the 1800s and sang those very old Negro spirituals like Swing Low Sweet Chariot and I want Jesus to Walk with me. I would feel like I was 4 years old in church in South Carolina somewhere. That's the only time I would have a recollection of being in the South as a child. I was about 5 years old when my father brought my family from South Carolina in 1957 to Brooklyn New York; yes that's right, we lived in Brooklyn for about 3 months with some of my father's family. My mother said that my father Moies left her with the children down South and promised her that he was going to New York City to make a way for them and come back to get us. She said a year later he came back with an old beat up truck and brought us to Brooklyn, New York to stay with some of his sisters and family.

CHAPTER 14

Well, here I was in 1999, now divorced and very little contact with my children and joining a new faith community. I had to leave William Institute Baptist Church on 132nd and 133rd St. and 7th avenue because that's the church my former wife and children were members of. God is great because during the experience of a very bitter divorce my heart was in so much pain because of how things turned out with my daughters. A sister at Canaan Baptist Church of Christ helped me to get a job through this brother name Mustafa at the Gloria Wise Boys and Girls Club After School Program in Coop City in the Bronx. In 1999, I met Janine who was about 8 years old and her sister Diva who was about 10 years old. They were participants in the after school program and the three of us became very good friends. It gave me a chance to transfer some of my fatherly emotions onto them because I was not allowed to interact with my 3 daughters. Janine and I became friends first because Janine would draw me these very nice pictures and Diva also begin to draw me pictures and give them to me. Diva's pictures were not as colorful as Janine's were but I never let her know it by my response to them. The three of us would be playing and laughing as friends. I needed them in my life and I came to learn that they also needed me in their lives because their father was not active in their lives also. Well, you know that eventually their mother and I started dating briefly; however, it was my relationship with Janine and Diva that helped me overcome the abandonment of my children. I enjoyed my time working at the Boys and Girls Club and had many fun filled days working from security to secretary to program coordinator. My best times there were when the Boys and Girls Club would send the staff for training and Seminars in other states. I went to Boston, Virginia, and Florida. The trips were weekend trips and after the trainings and seminars we would go out on the town and have us a very good time. There was one trip in Boston in 2002, we left the hotel looking for a disco to party and ended up at a club with the Aryan Brother Hood members. I recognized the scene right away because of my experience with them in the Federal system which I never had any problems with them mind you, but I knew that there could be a problem this night. The Aryan Brotherhood members were searching people before entering into the club. My 8 coworkers were in the van with me as the driver and they were mad as hell about the whole deal. They all had gotten their drink on and they were not used to these Boston White extremist denying them access into anything. I surrendered my life to God in 1988 and promised myself that I would never drink or drug ever again, because I was never the brightest apple in the barrel nor the sharpest tool in the box, and while under the influence of drugs and alcohol they made me that much more dumber and dull. I promised myself that drugs and alcohol would never ever again be a part of my life, and so, I now have some 15 years free from drugs and alcohol abuse. So here we were in 2002 in Boston facing the Aryan Brotherhood. I knew that we were not in any position to have a conflict with these guys and I did not want to get myself into trouble dealing with foolish people; because at the end of the day what ever happened we were sure to be made out to be the bad guys because we are Black and from New York City. I pushed all 8 of them back into the company van and we drove off and just as we were leaving the Police was coming with flashing lights and sirens screaming onto the scene. They did not pursue us but it was a very close call.

CHAPTER 15

In May of 1999, I received my first full year at Mercy College grade score and I had a 3.7 GPA as well as I made the Dean's List twice during my junior semester. I was proud as hell of myself because all these years' people called me crazy Larry from 122nd Street behind my back and now I'm in college with a 3.7 GPA. If God in the name of Jesus Christ can take an impulsive angry nut like Crazy Larry Love God and turn him around to obtain a 3.7 GPA then there is hope for anyone and everyone who wants to break the chains of self hatred and change their lives for the better. During my third semester I was confronted with this guy called Mathematics and his friend called the "Pygarian thorium", math and science kicked my butt, however, I was determined not to have to repeat any of my subjects so I sat up front in class, studied hard, asked questions, took good notes, turned in all assignments on time and made it out of math and science with a C grade which knocked my GPA down to a 3.3. While at Mercy College I had an opportunity to go to Rome in 2001 with other Mercy college students and faculty. I grew up watching those Roman movies and longed to see Rome. You see when I lived that life of self destruction and had lots of ill gotten fortune I was so afraid to leave Harlem for fear that I would miss something in Harlem so I hardly went anywhere. In fact during the 80s I visited New Orleans, New Mexico and California and that's it. However, now with only the income from my part time job and school refund money on a college trip to the ancient city of Rome where the Gladiators fought. We were there for a week and every time the students and faculty were heading in one direction, I was on my own heading in the opposite direction. I was so fascinated with Rome because as a kid my brother Kaye, homeboys Doug, Tony his brother Robert and Sister Donna and others spent hours at the West End movie theater on 125 street and Saint Nicholas and Morningside Avenue watching Gladiator movies with them fighting in the coliseum like Ben Hur. I was all over Rome and went to the Coliseum and called out all of my childhood friends and my brother's names that died and never got a chance to see life outside of 122 street. One day the professor who coordinated the trip stopped me in the hotel lobby and asked me "Larry are you enjoying yourself here in Rome". I thought it was an honest question because every time they went sightseeing I went in the opposite direction. I replied to her "professor here I stand this poor street kid from the streets of Harlem during some very hard times and now thanks to you I find myself in the ancient city of Rome, am I having a good time, hell I am having the time of my life and I thank you". We visited the Vatican and saw the Sistine Chapel Ceiling which was painted by Michel Angelo. It is a cornerstone work of high Renaissance art in the Vatican and it has scenes from the book of Genesis and visitors would observe its theological and temporal significance. Pope Julius the II commission the painting for the Papal Conclave. Our tour guide told us the story of Michel Angelo; while he was painting the Sistine Chapel ceiling he requested privacy. The Pope's clerk would often burst into the chapel to view Michel's work and it would make Michel mad as hell, so he painted the clerks facial image as one of the characters in the motif of the Catholics Theological belief of Heaven, Purgatory and Hell. Michel Angelo painted the clerk with Jackass ears and everyone who saw the painting know that it was the clerk's facial image. It was said that when the clerk saw the completion of the Sistine Chapel with an image of him in hell he ran to the Pope and demanded that the Pope make Michel Angelo take him out of hell and the Pope is said to have explain to the clerk "if he had placed you in Purgatory I could have prayed for you to come up to Heaven but not even the Pope can get you out of Hell," and the image of the clerk remains as part of the Sistine Chapel. I like the story and found it very impressive. The one thing that stood out to me was an image of a Black Pope of whom I did not get the name for some reason. However, I learned while studying for my Masters in theology at the New York Theological Seminary in 2012, that the father of Catholism is known to be Augustine of Hippo. Christopher Bellitto a church historian at Kean University in New Jersey said "North Africa was the Bible belt of early Christianity and Carthage was the buckle, he added referring to the City located in modern day Tunisia; so it should be no surprise that three early Popes hailed from that region: the 14th Pope, Victor (circa 189-198 A.D.); the 32nd Pope Miltiades (311-314 A.D.); and the 49th Pope, Gelasius (492-496 A.D.) were Black men. Davis said "the early Papacy was not white, it was much more diverse than one might think." I was excited and felt proud to see the black statue of the Black Pope; it made me feel a sense of belonging. On Wednesday we went back to the Vatican and saw Pope John Paul II, up close because on Wednesdays you can visit the Vatican for free and the Pope greets all visitors. I had a great time there and I have visited the city of Rome twice after my first experience. I had a wonderful time during my undergraduate experience at Mercy College. Looking back to the summer of 1974 when Zaytona begged me to leave Harlem and go to AT and T in North Carolina with her to enroll for college. I do understand that I was just not ready to believe in myself at that time. However, after being home for 3 years and moving from low paying jobs to lower paying jobs, I realized that I needed to get an education to better my chances for employment. So here I am attending Mercy College loving it and wishing I had the sense and presence of mind to have stayed in college years ago while serving time in Fiskill. In January of 2003 Mercy College gave a trip to Barcelona Spain where I walked the Las Ramblas and visited the Church of the Famiela. People were miming on Las Ramblas, and they were very good. There was one character acting as Charlie Chaplain and he had me laughing as he interacted with the moving traffic. At the water front is the statue of Christopher Columbus receiving the proclamation from Queen Isabella. History has painted a distorted account of Columbus as this great discoverer; but Christopher Minister who is a Latin American History Expert paints him in "The Truth about Christopher Columbus. Latin American History; Christopher Columbus wasn't his real name it was Cristotoro Colombo and he was born in Genoa Italy. He was a very religious man and a dedicated slave trader. Half of his voyages ended in disaster and he never believed he had found a new world. He was an economist and was only interested in getting paid. He was a great captain, but a terrible governor and was arrested and sent back to Spain." In Barcelona there is a church called The Church of the Famiela and it took about 100 years to build it. On one side of its facade are images of the Old Testament story and on the other side are images of the New Testament story.

One evening while walking the La Ramblas this older Spain Lady stopped me and began to curse me out for no reason in Spanish. I knew some of the Puertorican Spanish curse words but I was not able to recognize any of her Spanish. Some of my school mates came and a few of them were Spanish and they begin to tell me that the lady was cursing me out. My school mates were angry with her and I thought nothing of it; maybe it's because I was not able to understand what she was saying. However, it was after this experience that I began to understand the Spaniards prejudice towards Africans. When I looked up the history of Spain I learned that it was the Spaniards who had began the Transatlantic Slave trade. I then understood why all the African females that I saw in Spain where selling themselves on the streets of Spain like back in the 42nd street days of the 1960-70s in New York City when my brother Greg was a Pimp on 42nd Street. My brother Greg died in 1995 from HIV while I was in the Federal Prison system and they did not allow me to come to Greg and my sister Anne's funeral. I am told that my sister Anne began to stop drinking wine and was straightening her life up when she was hit and killed by a car while crossing the street on 134th St. and 8th avenue. Well, while visiting Spain, I never saw any of the African females working in the stores that I spent money in while there in Spain.

I like visiting Europe because as a kid lots of the movies I saw were filmed in parts of Europe and Europe seemed to be millions of miles out of my reach as a child, and now that I am able to visit and when the opportunity arrives I jump on the chance to do so. I feel that at some point in my life I must make my pilgrimage to Africa one day. However, when I see from the News about all the turmoil going on in many of the African countries that appear to be perpetuated by African leaders, I continue to long for the day when I can visit a nation in Africa that is in peace with its own people. It's something within my soul that longs for me to visit Africa and God willing I will one day. I am clear that out of all the places that I have traveled to like the Caribbean's, Rome, Spain, Paris France, London England, Hawaii are all nice places to visit but as an African American male I rather live my life here in America where African Americans and other minorities are treated unfairly by the ruling party, but yet in that unfair treatment I find it better than how Blacks are treated in many other places that I have visited. The truth be told I only have a right to claim America as my home because this is the land that my ancestors built from the ground up for 400 years of free hard labor under the cruel whip of slavery, and Jim Crow. America always brag about their quick rise to power and dominance over the world without ever mentioning the fact that it was from the 400 years of free labor which allowed America to obtain superiority over others. My father served in World War II in the United States Navy and when he got out of the Navy he was denied all military benefits that White Soldiers received so freely. Not only did my people build America with free labor, but they bled and died just as much if not more than anyone else claiming to be Americans. I believe that we owe it to our ancestors to always live and thrive in the land they died building for free so that their pain from working sun up till sun down labor would not be in vain; as well as our presence serves as a quiet reminder to America that their unjust deeds will always stand looking into their souls and seeing them for what they really are.

When I think about all that my ancestors endured here in North America, I think of the brutality they lived with and wonder if they ever had any hope of some day being saved by others from Africa coming to set them free. When singing the Negro Anthem and the part that says "when hope unborn had died", my ancestors had nothing or no one to hope for freedom from; so they embraced the God that their slave masters enforced upon them to believe in which was the Greco Roman view of God. They were told that God made them slaves but they learned through the Theology of Jesus Christ that God does not want anyone to be another person's slave.

As a troubled youth on the streets of Harlem we had discussions about Africa and about our brothers and sisters there. As kids, we had trouble trying to understand why no one had attempted to free us from the hands of Massa. Yes, as a child I was always in trouble and could not read, but I had a sense of my blackness from James Brown teaching us to "Say it loud, I am black and I am proud", and there was brother Malcolm X teaching us to embrace our God given right to stand as Black Men and not the boy that Massa wanted us to be. I was so disappointed when Africans began to migrate to America in large numbers during the late 1970s-2000. I wanted so much to learn about them and their culture because they were my long lost brothers and sisters. My disappointment came as they settled in and began to distant themselves from African Americans and act as if they were better than the very people who made it possible for them to come to America. As our ancestors forced America to change its position through the Civil Rights movements of African Americans and yet they think they're better. One day in 1997 I had a very interesting conversation with an African Cab driver and he was telling me how he thought African Americans were lazy and dumb because they had not made any economic impact into the social structure of America, and if he had been in America as long as Black Americans had, he would have been far more successful. I said to him stick around and let's have this discussion after you have been in America about 20 years. This discussion made me think about the days when many Black churches in America would have fund raisers to send money to Africa to assist them with clean water and agriculture. We now hear this colonized brain washed African cab driver looking down on the very people who made it possible for him to be in America without chains on his feet. Had it not been for our ancestors, willingness to march and boycott whenever injustice to people of color even this brain washed African driving me crazy with his distorted impression of American equality for all. Here he sits judging the very people who has endured inequality from Masor for some 400 plus years to this very date. Here we are today in our Black Churches and I no longer hear fund raising for Africa and I wonder if it has anything to do with the Africans that migrated in the 70s-2000 and are here living separated from African Americans as well as it was rumored that the money was not going where it was supposed to.

CHAPTER 16

Yes, America is my Country and I am proud to be an American for it is the land that I love even if it pretends that it does not see me when I walk by. I walk with an air of privilege throughout my America and I demand the same service my White Americans receive. The thought has often occurred to me the reason the numerical number 13 is often equated as bad luck. When I think of why the number 13 is equated as bad luck, I also think of the Black Cat which is often spoken of as a symbol of bad luck and then I think of the African American people and how they seem to be painted with the same stigma as the unlucky 13 and the Black Cat by some unfair Rembrandt impersonator. It is said that the numerical number 13 became the unlucky number based upon the biblical character of Judas one of the 12 disciples of Jesus. It's not sure why Judas was distinguished during the Last Supper as the 13th person present at the table however the conspiracy to make the numerical number 13 the unlucky number has its origin at the Last Supper of Jesus. Mind you again, no one knows what order Judas sat in during the Last Supper but that's where the number 13 became unlucky. I would like to now consider the number 13 and the African American and how the American culture, diabolical attempt to mark them as one in the same. The 13th floor in a high-rise of America is like the Black man living in America, he is there in plain sight just as the 13th floor is in the high-rise building from the outside of the building, but it is treated as if it does not exist. A high-rise building with 15 floors or more does not give notice to the 13th floor in most high-rises. It is not counted in the elevator or on the floor, yet the 13th floor is clearly there in the construction of the high-rise. The builders of the high-rise refuse to identify the 13th floor or add its number in accordance to its proper numerical order in the elevator and on the floors of the building. The number 13 becomes either the 14th floor or the 15th floor so the high-rise is constructed on a level of the first floor to the 12th floor and then the 14th or the 15th floor and all other floors within the building. However when you look up at the high-rise and you begin to count the floors from the number one to its highest level of the building, one must count the number 13 floor after reaching the number 12 numerically or your count is incorrect. So to the American Black man has always been treated like unlucky 13. In America the Black man stands tall strong intelligent and brave hearted, but is told by others that he is inferior, unintelligent and weak hearted; the Black man is oppressed and forced to live his life just like the unlucky 13th floor of a high-rise. He stands just as tall and secure as all the (men) floors in the building but yet, the American Black male goes unnoticed in America because he is not accepted for the content of his character just as the 13 floor of the high rise is not counted in its proper numerical order. In America, in the year 2016, with an African-American president of the United States serving two terms as Commander in Chief of these United States, and the American Black male is forced to continue to live an invisible life unnoticed and overlooked to the point of today's American Black male could possibly be on the verge of extinction due to a number of negative social factors created by not being counted correctly in its humanitarian order of belonging. In America the African American male has lots of forces eating away at them, such as the Jim Crow Prison Industry, premeditated inferior education system, indoctrinated sense of hopelessness if I can't sing like

Michael Jackson, fight like Mike Tyson are slam duck like Michael Jordan to entertain Masor. There is also the Black to Black killings and Black males being gun down by Law Enforcement (Police) who have this racial ideology that African American lives does not matter and they can use as much force as they feel moved to use with legal impunity; these factors cause African American males to be few and fare between. What hurts the most is when the police kills an unarmed Black male in 2016, and gives the same excuses to justify the unfair killing as during the lynching of African Americans in America when they lynched 14 years old Emmett Till and thousands of others with such reasons like "He whistled at a white woman, and as the police was scared for his life he shot the unarmed nigger in the back." So to the 13th floor has been conditioned to not see itself as an important part of the internal structure of the high-rise and the number 13 has been forced to accept its inferior position within the high-rise and is unable to see that all floors above it is dependent upon the 13th floor standing strong and tall no matter what number it's called outside of its numerical order because if the 13th floor gives in all floors above it will crash down and the high-rise will become destroyed.

As the 13th number represents so many different symbolisms we think back to the 13 colonies, the number one meaning knowledge, and the number three meaning wisdom and when you add one and three together it equals four which means culture or freedom from a mathematic prospective. So the Black man, the invisible Black man, must learn to embrace the reality that he/she is just as strong intelligent and brave hearted as any other human being that walks the face of the earth and give the number 13 its rightful place in the numerical order of calculations knowing that mathematics got its beginning from the Egyptians and that there is no number in the numerical order that is a bad luck number. All numbers are equal to one another because they are all equal in their own right. So to my American Black People, I say up you mighty nation rise up and stand with your shoulders held strong and firm and your head held high looking straight ahead knowing that God did not create any unlucky group of people and as America's founding fathers stumbled upon a fact of reality when in the constitution it reads " We hold these truths to be self-evident, that all men (and women) are created equal, that they are endowed by their Creator with certain Rights, that among these are Life, Liberty and the pursuit of Happiness." So my Brothers and Sisters lets love one another with open arms of care and concern for each other because we are each other's keeper and we are responsible for what happens to our Race of African American people and all others of humanity.

While at Mercy College in 2000, it became time for me to select a major and I decided to major in Social Work because I wanted to help the young Larry Loves of the world that grow up fatherless and filled with anger because of it. I wanted to be in a position to help our children not fall head long into the state of despair and of self hate leading to destruction like I wallowed in for some 35 years of life. I was also looking for answers as to reasons why so many of the males from my community and others like mine made such poor life choices and suffered so harshly. My first class was at the Dobbs Ferry Campus in Ardsley New York and the professor pulled me to the side the first day of class and informed me that because I was a freshman I should not have been allowed to enroll into the Social Work course at this time of my schooling. She suggested that I drop the Social Work course. I respectfully informed her that I don't drop any classes that I registered to major in. She gave me this strange look and then said "Ok", to stay in this course you have to write an essay." That was my first time writing an essay on the spot and after I wrote it the professor said "okay, you can stay in the course".

I found it very interesting as I learned from the White prospective about the social dynamics of humanity, and how lots of the dysfunctions within communities did not just drop in, out of the clear blue sky, but that those in power made extra efforts to make sure that poverty, illiteracy, drugs, disparity and self hate coexisted in 122nd street and other communities like mine. There were so many people that grew up with me that died or was sent to prison for years because of these dynamics plaguing our community. I often wondered what might, America look like if the Johnny Kaye's, Gregory's, Douglas, Apple Jacks, Sisters, Cookies and so many others did not make such poor choices that led to their early deaths. Suppose they went to school and received a quality education; what jobs would there be for them and would it be enough jobs available because I am talking about millions of young people in the 1960s through 1996 that died from gun violence and drug related deaths. Once Dr. Martin Luther King was savagely assassinated in April of 1968, drugs became available on every corner of the Harlem community and for the most part it looks like Law enforcement had turned a blind eye to all the drug dealing done in the open streets of Harlem and other communities. Yes, there was occasional arrest made throughout Harlem. They had the nerve to even put the diabolical plot on the Big Screen in the movie The God Father when they had the seen where all five mafia families meet to agree about who will control what and they said in the movie, which has nothing to do with the Mafia's prospective, just what the seen pointed out "keep the drugs in the Black communities because they don't have any souls". Every so often there would be a French Connection like arrest of some 300 key loads of heroin and they would point to the Mafia as the perpetrators of the crime, but I am here as a former African American Black Gangster, to tell you that from the 1960s through 1990s the drug thirst for Heroin, Cocaine and Marijuana was so massive in America that the French Connection like drug bust were nothing but a distraction from who the real drug dealers in America were back then and are today to me.

The hunger for drugs at the time could never have been quenched by some small organized crime family. The American drug thirst was quenched by an entity that was able to deliver ship loads of drugs to America on a daily basis and I be darn if little big mafia was able to deliver ship loads of drugs on a daily basis to the greatest nation in the world and all of its security. I Larry, who Loves God, Moses Coldwell proclaim that those in power in America along with the American government played the biggest part in supplying America with enough Heroin, Cocaine, and Marijuana to satisfy the hunger for drugs because it met their social population control as well as it was the biggest grossing commodity on the Stock Exchange at the time and still stands true to the writing of this book. Let's remember the Alexander Haig trial when it was said "America brought us (Contras) plane loads of guns and in return we gave them plane loads of Cocaine to take back to America (Secret ties between CIA, drugs revealed by Rosalind Muhammad), also know that the CIA has supported the production of opium production and exporting heroin (1950-1970s, Southeast Asia: Drug Lords and Covert Wars by Alfred McCoy, Professor of Southeast Asian history, University of Wisconsin). Today in 2016, we now have the American Government convincing Americans that Marijuana is socially acceptable and is in the same group today as alcohol. It benefits the Government when its majority of citizens are socially distracted and Marijuana will surely keep them laughing, sleeping and as dumb as it had me while America continues to mess up the economy and environment for that one percent's best benefit. I learned that my community suffered from a lack of knowledge which reminds me of a Bible verse that reads "my people are destroyed for lack of knowledge" (Hosea 4:6a KJV). There we were in Harlem and other communities not knowing that the easy access to drugs were put there and allowed to be there for our detriment intentionally. There was one time in about 1970 when the Mayor I believe and others during the so called "War on Drugs", had all these kilos of drugs and they was going to burn them in front of the Theresa Hotel on 125th Street and 7th avenue. It's the same hotel that Fidel Castro stayed at in Harlem when he visited America on his Honey Moon in 1948, which is 2 blocks from 122nd St. Fidel was denied lodging in the hotels down town so he stayed in Harlem. I like one of his many quotes when he said "Marxism what society was" and it means "I was like a blindfolded man in a forest, who doesn't even know where north or south is. If you don't eventually come to truly understand the history of the class struggle, or at least have a clear idea that society is divided between the haves and the have not's, and that some people subjugate and exploit other people, you're lost in a forest, not knowing anything" (Fidel Castro on discovering Marxism, 2009[28]. As they burned the drugs while I stood there watching them burn the drugs you never smelled anything burning. I was able to identify and understand that the social norms of my community from the teachings in school as I majored in Social Work, I learned how to recognize the diabolical plots to cripple or destroy those that are less fortunate than those in Super Power.

Hope unborn was still dead in my community and all we could focus on was one another in our desperation to survive. Here we were living in an all out war zone and our block could have been one of the major battle fields at the time when we were being blasted with bombs of drug addiction, illiteracy, poverty, self hate and hopelessness within our community. Yes, there was a war going on and the people of 122nd street did not know that they were on one of the main battle fields being fired upon by the enemy. From my past experience with the devastation of drugs in my community I wonder just what in the world is going on today in 2019 with the fight to legalize drugs that has killed so many of my siblings and people from my community. In 1960s through 1970s Huey Newton, George Jackson, Angela Davis and others tried to wake us up as political solders for the people; the Black Panthers and the BLA (Black Liberation Army). However, Jay Edger Hoover the head of the FBI quickly squashed out the Black Panther Party so quickly until most of us did not even know that they were fighting to free us from the physical and psychological suppression of the ruling party. Those sisters and brothers in the Black Panther Party were political soldiers and we still have some of them incarcerated to this very date from trying to liberate us from the oppression of the ruling party. We have brothers like Daruber Moore and Dr. Matula Sukar and others that are still in prison and denied parole because the government wants us to believe that they were just common criminals and deserve to be in prison for the rest of their lives. Shame on America, because those soldiers are political prisoners and they deserve to be set free after spending 30 plus years in America's Jim Crow Industrialized Prison System.

In the year 2003 I graduated with a 3.5 GPA Bachelor degree in Social Work and was told by the dean of social work that I would not be allowed to sit for the licensed exam due to my past criminal record. I heard her, but I did not believe her because one of the primary principles of Social Work is to restore a person or community to a healthy and fair level of social stability and giving people fair and equal opportunity for growth and development. Therefore, it was no way in the world, the NASW or anyone else would be able to deny me if I qualified to sit for the exam. So, I set my sights on obtaining my Masters in Social Work and from there to obtain my license. My focus was on obtaining my LMSW because throughout all my criminal experience I was standing in the court room and they would say "the United States of America against Larry Coldwell" and now I have the possibility to obtain my Social Work License by the New York State Board of Education, made me feel and believe that I can put my past criminal behavior far behind me and that I have arrived as a citizen of the United States of America.

I joined Prison Ministry in Canaan Baptist Church of Christ in 2001, and I love to see the looks on the inmates at Riker's Island and Eastern Correctional Facility face, when doing Prison Ministry and I tell them about my education and the possibility of becoming a Licensed Social Worker. Their faces light up with hope and possibility and they look at me with a sense of pride for me and the accomplishments I have achieved. I have heard a number of them say to me "Brother Larry if you can do it so can I", and my response would be "you sure can". I encourage the inmates that I visit to bring their good habits home with them when they make parole; because as inmates one acquires very good habits like eating healthy, working out, reading positive books and socializing in positive intellectual conversations and most of all a working relationship with a God of their understanding, oh yes, and a drug free life. The drug free life is not because they are in prison and no drugs are available because in all the prisons I have served time in there was always enough drugs for a person to get high with to the point of becoming addicted if they had the money to buy it, and wanted to. The good habits that some inmates have acquired are making better life choices that will keep them focused on obtaining their goals when they return home.

When I was in the Federal Prison system I made up my mind that I would follow the prison rules and that if I can stay out of trouble while in prison, then I could stay out of trouble when I came home from the Jim Crow Industrialized Prison System. I thank the God of my understanding in the holy name of Jesus Christ that to this day it has worked, because I have been home crime and trouble free for the last 24 years of writing this book. I stopped smoking marijuana and drinking cheap champagne as I asked myself "Larry why do you smoke and drink and my answer was because I know that the life as a American Black Gangster had consequences that I would have to one day pay for my behavior so I smoked and drunk alcohol to drown out that reality". I made up my mind that I was not going to use any drugs and alcohol any more in my life while in prison in the year 1989. I also stopped eating red meat, pork and I surrendered my life to the God of my understanding. I also started fasting from 12PM Sunday night till 12PM Monday night I don't eat or drink anything and from 12PM Monday night till 12Noon Tuesday I only drink juices and water and on Wednesday, Thursday and Fridays for breakfast, I eat five pieces of fruit and a hand full of nuts and I workout on Wednesday, Thursday and Fridays. I acquired these good habits while in prison and I continue to live this way for these last 24 years of FREEDOM from mass incarceration. My doctor said for my age I am the healthiest person he has met. I also don't cheat on my wife because I promised myself that I would be true to my wife and I learned from those other relationships when my loyalty was misplaced and I messed up my first marriage by cheating on her with people that only wanted what I had financially and physically. So I continue to walk hand in hand with the God of my understanding in the name of Jesus Christ, every day. The good habits inmates acquire while incarcerated when applied to their daily lives when out of prison will help them to stay focus on their goals and objectives, leading to a life free of substance abuse and free of Jim Crow Industrialization, as well as a healthy life.

CHAPTER 17

In February of 2003, my children's mother asked to get back together after her boyfriend died in 2002. When she asked me, I thought for a second to say some mean and ugly things to her because of the hurt I hold to this day from the poor relationship I have with my twin daughters, but instead I just said "I'm sorry but that is not where my mind is." Again, I don't blame her for any of the ugliness of our divorce, it's just how things turned out and I would love to be able to say "hello, how are you" to her in passing and mean every word of it; because I should have been the man to her then that I am today. I was such a immature fool during our early days of marriage. I learned from my first marriage to be true and loyal to my partner because other woman that are looking for a mate will gladly cheat with you on your wife due to the extreme shortage of Black men due to incarceration and other predators feeding off of the few Black men within America's society. You see it's not the woman who is cheating when she sleeps with a married man, it's the married man that is cheating on his word to be faithful and true to his partner the one that he becomes one with during their intimate moments. Also the woman has sexual needs and it's difficult to find a mate due to the shortage of men and here I come along thinking I am God's gift to every woman that will say yes to my cheating ways. The single woman will go along with the cheating relationship because she knows that if anything happens to you she has no investment in you and she is free to just walk away; also she is possibly jealous of the wife's position of being married to the cheater and so she takes the position of "let his wife take care of his dumb butt," leaving you the cheater in prison or in a hospital needing someone to show you love and the only person that will more times than not be there visiting you is the wife whom you have been cheating on. I also learned that to cheat on your partner is to give another woman the competitor power over your wife and that is what hurts the wife to the core of her soul more than anything else the cheater does. Therefore I continue to be focused on my relationship because at the end of the day a cheater only really cheats on himself.

In 2004 life was going very well for me and I noticed this sister in church on a Sunday sitting in the balcony section where I sat. I was not that interested in her because I thought she had big feet. She was in the Dance the Word Ministry at Canaan and one Sunday when she was ministering God revealed her to me as a African Queen, I had never saw her in that light before. Well on this day I saw her as my African Queen and I never noticed her big feet after that day. I shared with a few of our Prison Ministry sisters that I was interested in her and they assured me that Harriett which is her name would not give me the time of day. I told Steve about her and asked him "don't Harriett look like an African Queen" and he said "no she don't". I said to myself maybe to him she doesn't but to me she sure looks like my African Queen. I pursued her and began courting her. Yes, I grew up courting sisters that I wanted to have a meaningful relationship with. I asked her mother who also goes to Canaan "if I could add to the Sunshine in her daughter's life." Her mother said "it's alright with me." This was the first time out of two other meaningful relationships I have had that a mother did not mind if I courted her daughter. My children's mother's mother and Zaytona's mother could not stand the thought of me courting their daughters. I must admit that they had every right to their feelings because at that time I was considered the worst guy on the block as crazy as I was; so I have learned to understand their feelings at that time. However, I am reminded of this Gospel song that says "He (God) saw the best in me when everyone around me could only see the worst in me." Here I was courting my African Queen. My twin daughters stop speaking to me shortly after I had informed their mother that I was not interested in rekindling our marriage. They would walk pass me in church and made sure they spoke to all the men in church except their father. They attended Canaan a few months before their mother asked me to get back together with her. Levesa, my oldest daughter hardly came to Canaan and when she did she would speak to her father. Because of my twins, Steve and I relationship begin to change at this point because my twins begin to manipulate him to come between them and me. I tried talking to him about it but he came across as if he did not care about my pain as long as he could walk away as the hero. I was never invited to any of my twin daughters graduations from Junior High School or High School nor College but Steve was and he went and kept it a secret from me. I tried to explain to him that as a lifelong friend, look like to me that every time they invited him to something like that he should have asked them if they invited their father or communicate with me that he was invited and not sneak around my back playing my role and again he showed no interest as long as he was able to play the hero part. I would never just show up at any of their functions because when they graduated from Pre School I figured out when and the school told me where it would be held at and I showed up uninvited in 1999 and my three daughters, their mother and her boy friend were there taking pictures and laughing and when I stepped from behind the glass door all the laughing stopped and everyone were looking at me as if I had just broke into their house while they were around the dinner table celebrating a family reunion. I had three envelopes with $150 for each of them and no one said hello so I just passed out the, envelops to them and just walked away quietly. No one said thank you that I was able to hear. I was never so hurt in my life and for some reason I did not feel the full impact of the hurt because I had on sunglasses it was a very sunny day and I think the glasses reflected some of the pain of rejection and hatred I felt coming from my own children unfairly. I wanted to cry that day in June of 1999 as I walked away but again the sunglasses reflected the full impact of the moment from me and I could not cry after wanting to. I promised myself that day that if I was not invited by them to attend one of their special moments then I would not intrude on their time for fear of being hurt as deeply as I was that day. All three of them have gone on to graduate from Junior High and High School and I was never invited and I never tried to go. In 2007 Levesa graduated from School Safety Academy and invited me and I gladly went. My second daughter graduated from Corrections Officer Academy in 2013 and I was not invited, but Steve was and he kept it a secret from me just as they did and again when I asked him why does he allow my children to manipulate him to come between me and them he acted like he felt that I got what I deserved and again he was able to ride off into the Sunset looking like the hero at my expense.

In 2007 my beautiful Queen and I decided to get married and I moved in with Harriett so that we could save up for the wedding which was scheduled for September 2008. I thank God for my wife to be and her family for they have been very kind and tolerant of me throughout the years. Harriett and I were married on September 5, 2008 on a Friday at Canaan Baptist Church by Pastor Francis and Steve was my best man, yes, Steve the hero was my best man, with Pee Wee, Augie, Avery and my God brother Greg as my best men. We wrote our own wedding vows and our reception was at the Villa Barone in the Bronx. We had a ball at the reception, Harriett and I came up out of the floor into the Ballroom to Shaft by Isaac Hayes. My Mother in Law was very supportive of our union emotionally and financially. When Harriett and I began dating, I inherited one of the nicest nine years old boys as a nephew I had ever met in my life. He knew the transit system just as good as the MTA map and he could navigate you from New York City to Florida by way of I95, better than any adult I know. Harriett and I cruised to Europe for our honeymoon the very next day of our wedding and again I visited the Vatican for a few days. When I take a trip I often think about that so called Gangster life I once lived and all the money that was made and how I never enjoyed any of it as well as hardly went anywhere from Harlem other than to the Bronx, and now I travel all over the world with my little bit of hard earned working 9 to 5 job money visiting wonderful places in this world, and I have a great time when I get there.

In June of 2009 I graduated from Adelphi University with my Masters degree in Social Work and I just knew that the world would not use my past to hold me back. My focus was to obtain a job in a hospital setting as a Social Worker. I was so proud of myself standing with my Masters degree after not learning how to read until I was 15 years old in Warwick State training school. I wish I could remember the teacher name that asked me if I wanted to learn how to read, and sorry that I can't, what I do remember is that he was of African American decent. Well, just as I got over the hurdle of obtaining my Masters degree, I learned that I would have to obtain my License in Social Work before the world would take notice. So I set out to acquire my license and took training courses causing me about 5,000.00 in study material to prepare for the four hour exam, I would press finish and it would come up "failed" at the end of the exam. I got to the point that I begin to doubt myself and wondered if I would ever pass the exam; mind you there has been a protest against the Social Work exam because it is geared to the psychological thinking of white Americans and not the minority Americans psychological thinking. However, I refused to give up on my goal in life.

In 2009 I began having difficulty holding down employment. I was working as s case manager on one job in October and was terminated in 8 days because the site director told me I did not know where my loyalty belonged. She thought I was sent to spy on her site for another person that had her hire me. A few months later I worked as a House Manager Supervisor and I was fired in 25 days and was told by the founder of the program that I make his heart hurt. I was told weeks later by someone working there that there were smiling back stabbers at my success in changing the culture of the agency and they poisoned my name to the director. What I have trouble understanding is that all of these participants are Black like me, yet they will see me without a job for little to no real reason.

I eventually landed a nice job in a Mentor program called In Arms Reach, Inc. the founder and CEO is Terrance his mother's family and I was raised together in 122nd street. I had a great time there and gave it my very best shot. I came to work every day on time and I followed through with all directives from Terrance and there was a large growth in Mentees and Mentors during my employment there. The funding ran out 2 years later and my position was closed due to funding so I was told.

I continued to sit for my license and on my 13th test I finally passed the exam, and ran out into the hallway and got down on my knees to thank my God in the holy name of Jesus Christ. My dream and goal was to obtain my license for my dream job working in a hospital setting as a Licensed Master Social Worker. So here I stand now as a LMSW in 2013, and I passed my resume around to every hospital in the Bronx and Manhattan with no one showing any interest in hiring me. I wanted to obtain my Doctorate in Social Work but something within me moved me to enroll into New York Theological Seminary, mind you I have no desire to be any ones Pastor and yes, I do preach to the brothers at Eastern Correctional Facility when we visit for Prison Ministry. I don't like preaching a sermon where the key verses are used to get people excited. I believe in bringing a message that will stimulate the hearers' intellect causing them to rethink about their life choices and improve on their future choices to bring about empowerment and change in their lives. That something which moved me to go to Seminary is that same quiet voice that I heard when Levesa was sick and when I was moved to call Bingo for our seniors. I graduated in May of 2015, with my Masters in Theology, and I tell you I have had an eye opening faith jolting experience and yet I walk away believing in God the Creator in the holy name of Jesus Christ. My reason for this position is that, I come to believe that none of us know for sure about the true concept of God the Creator. Therefore if my neighbor believes in another way of viewing God its fine with me because no matter what humanity's perspective of God is, if it is not embedded in "Doing Justly, Loving, Mercy, and walking humbly before your God" (Micah 6:8 KJV), I ask what good is your God to humanity anyway? We take that whole God view and treat each other like kids playing in the school yard sounding like "nana nana, my god is better than your god". It reminds me of kids arguing over whose baseball is the best or who can jump the highest. Today I conclude that God of the universe will not allow frail humanity to know for certain who are what God is because the minute any of us know for sure we are subject to pollute it and manipulate it to our own selfish narcissistic advantage; in the same way as we have done everything on God's earth to this very date.

    I believe that if we do justice, show love and mercy to one another as well as respect the fact that there is a creator in the world we would all make it into Nirvana.

    As I consider my employment challenges and the so few Black Men I see heading to work, I ask the question where are the Black

Men, and why is it that so few of us find meaningful employment? Just as I asked this question I am sadly reminded that when I visit the prison system and its New Jim Crow industrialized system I look out at the inmates I am ministering to and there are all my missing Black Men serving long prison sentences with a 90% White prison guards system for self destructive behavior within our communities.

I look today at the violence perpetrated against each other by our youth and I wonder how have we become so over flowing with self hatred. Our youth who perpetrates these acts of shooting one another just because you have a gun and hate the image of yourself that you see in your brother causes me to scratch my head in amazement. Here they are at the age of 14-25 years old born and raised within 5 city blocks of each other and now as teenagers we will not hesitate to pick up a gun and shoot in a crowd of our own people for absolutely nothing. But, if the truth be told we all have gone to the same school together and grow up playing in the same parks as youth. But now at 17 years old with their pants hanging off their butts, and a borrowed gun that they have absolutely no experience shooting. They stand with their butt out eyes closed shooting in a crowd of people that live 3 blocks from their block because they are beefing over who is the bad mother, when all of them are soft cowards who can't wait to snitch when you're caught for your madness. Yes, that's how I see you snitching. If there is any of our youth reading this part of my book I challenge you to ask yourself the question "why do I hate myself to the point that I will kill anyone that looks like me." Yes, there was a time in my life when I had that same self hatred and I to found myself hurting my brother for reminding me how Black I look. However, one day thank God I learned to love myself and from that day forward I could no longer hurt others for reminding me of my Blackness in a world where if your White your all right and if your Brown you can stick around, but if your Black like me then you have to get the hell back. I got me an education and said to myself I AM BLACK AND I AM PROUD OF MY BLACKNESS, and for those who will not give me a fair chance I say later for them because I refuse to hurt my brothers and sisters as well as myself and anyone else just because the Man will not give me a chance to earn my living.

When will we wake up and forgive our selves enough to begin to love one another for just being an African American Black person. When I'm watching TV today and the news anchor introduce a crime seen the first thing I say to myself is "please don't let it be a black person that's the perpetrator," and almost always its Black and more times than not I am disappointed because it's a Black person most of the time. Our Black professionals like Actors, Athletes and entertainers are going to prison today for crimes that White entertainers hardly ever go to prison for like taxes and personal drug possession. Yet, when Wall Street cheated America out of Billions of dollars not one of those bankers or corporations went to prison except a guy whose name just so happen to be **Madeof,** when Greenspan was supposed to be watching out for cheaters as the head of the treasury. Have you ever heard of White Athletes going to prison for shooting themselves in the leg. America will imprison a Black person for crimes that White people get a pass on when caught every day. We as American Blacks are caught in a web of self destruction because we are only concerned with our own individual needs. The Athlete that shot himself in the leg would have never used that gun on a White person and I am not implying hurt anyone, I am just making the point that a gun in a black person's hands will only be used to hurt his own people; the actor that went to prison for tax evasion turned his back on his community who supported him in his beginning career and did not offer to help his community when he thought he had arrived. Well, that's what the other guy did in the late 70s and they did not rest until his butt was in prison serving time. How about the negative Rap music that teach us how to hate our Blackness to the point that they sing about killing the nigger who steps on their sneakers, in a crowd of people. As long as those songs degrade Blacks it will surely receive a Grammy; I often wonder how many Grammies would that Rapper win, if the lyrics of the songs were degrading another race of people other than their own. It took me a long time of incarceration to learn that we can't do things that others can do and get away with it, they will make us pay harsher punishment even if we think we are not Black but yet have 10 % of Black blood in us.

We as African Americans must wake up and look around us because everyone that has come to our country within the past 15 years appear to be making economic gains exceeding us and if we don't make better life and community choices 20 years from now our children can find themselves working those same jobs at the same salary that undocumented people are working today. Young brothers and sisters you had better get in school and obtain a quality education or trade or start a business and support each other and last of all, you had better get these old sellout Colored politicians because they are helping the controlling powers keep you oppressed as they encourage you to get out and vote for them. Our Black youth must learn the political system and start running for office today, if they hope to bring about change for the better.

I continue to seek employment with a Masters degree and run smack dab into my Jim Crow unconscious brothers and sisters. I had this job recently and it lasted about 3 weeks. I was terminated because "we don't think you would be able to solve the staff's concerns if they should have one and brought it to your attention for a remedy". Lord being a conscious Black Man sure does make me want to holler and throw up both my hands at times; but I guess I am too stupid to give up. Thus I continue to look to the God of my understanding in the name of Jesus Christ as my source for deliverance from unfair treatment by my own people when it comes to employment; after all Jesus brought me out of a much darker place when he broke the sin chains that had me bound for some 30 years. Yes, it's hard as hell for a Black Man in America to up lift himself after making the foolish mistakes I made as an angry confused self hatred young man, but again I rise like that sister Maya Angelou said to do, I rise.

So during church service I became aware that my people are very connected to their spirituality and I like to think that it dates back to the time when our ancestors had to pick cotton from sun up until sun down and had nothing to believe in but their faith in God in the name of Jesus Christ for deliverance from the jaws of White imposed hateful slavery. Such a place leaves one to feel hopeless and the only relief one has is when we look to God to lift the heavy heels of the slave master from off our backs. Today I feel so in kinship with my ancestors as I continue to struggle with obtaining meaningful employment.

I continue to find myself with a job for a few weeks and without a job very soon after. On August 7, 2013, I sat again for my license and PASSED my exam. Boy was I happy and thankful to God. I was so glad to have passed the exam until I wanted to walk home from Connecticut where I took the test. It took me 2 hours to compose myself before I begin driving back to the Boogie down Bronx Riverdale section. However, two weeks later I received a letter stating that because of my criminal past, I must appeal to the New York State board of Education for their approval to be granted my License. Well, here I go again, because of my poor life choices I must fight like hell to receive what I earned honestly. So I got reference letters and wrote a letter requesting my License and in September 2013, I was granted my LMSW by the New York State Board of Education and I was very proud and wished my Mother could have been alive to see it because until that date all I ever received from the New York State was a prison sentence.

I ran out with my License and my resume filling out applications as an LMSW to every hospital in Harlem and the

Bronx as well as Nursing Homes I could think of. I knew that my employment issues was over and in October 2013, I was hired in a Shelter program and had the worst job experience ever, causing me to see a therapist for six weeks. My ideal job has been in a hospital setting as a Social Worker or a Nursing Home and I have yet to obtain such a position. There times in my life when I briefly feel like God has forgotten about me and that no one gives a dam about my plight. However, when I think about the goodness of the God of my understanding and all that I have accomplished I know that I just have to keep trying. The only problem with keep trying is that I am aging out of employment and I am afraid that when it comes time to retire I will not have enough credits for a decent benefit package. As I write, my life story, I am gainfully employed as a License Master Social Worker and looking forward to the day when I can retire.

When I think back to my days as an angry youth because his daddy was not on the scene and all the harm I did to myself I wish I was not so angry and that I made better life choices as a youth.

If there's anyone reading this book that feels like I did for whatever reason I ask you to please find a way to forgive who so ever it is from the heart, so that you can free yourself from all the anger and learn to make better life choices for yourself.

To the street hustler, I beg of you to wake up and know that you're being played by a street game that has no success stories. Don't give the prison system your best employment years because you deserve better and nothing in that life is worth your freedom.

When I talked about White people in this book, I am not talking about my White neighbor. I am talking about those that are in power and make these rules that are so unfair to all of society.

To those of you that have a relationship with a God of your understanding I encourage you to never stop believing in your God, and respect others and their spiritual beliefs and to allow others to believe in the God of their understanding as long as your

God is based upon love and care for all of humanity, as we accept others for who they are and not whom we think they should be. God of all creation is waiting for humanity to operate from the spirit of love, mercy and compassion towards all of humanity in the same manner as we do with our dogs, cats and other animals.

Can you please tell me who raised that crazy Larry who now loves God?

Thank you Jesus for saving my soul, when those correction officers came to kill me that night, when he saw my face he saw your face of mercy, causing him to walk away with the other correction officers because the Lord was not done with me yet. Dear God, you turned my life all the way around for the better and you put my world upside down for the much better. I have learned to love me and never turn back to that ungodly life I once lived.

I know I have been changed to the point that my God allowed me to clean up what I messed up, and now live a second life in the holy name of Jesus Christ the God of my understanding.

THE END

www.ingramcontent.com/pod-product-compliance
Ingram Content Group UK Ltd.
Pitfield, Milton Keynes, MK11 3LW, UK
UKHW022226230426
12048UKWH00016BA/1095